Campus Ministry

The Church Beyond Itself

Donald G. Shockley

Westminster/John Knox Press
LOUISVILLE

Unless otherwise indicated, Scripture quotations are from the Revised Standard Version of the Holy Bible, copyright, 1946, 1952, and © 1971, 1973 by the Division of Christian Education, National Council of the Churches of Christ in the U.S.A. and used by permission.

Acknowledgment is made for permission to reprint from the following sources:

To the U.S. Catholic Conference for excerpt from "Empowered by the Spirit: Campus Ministry Faces the Future." © 1986, U.S. Catholic Conference, Washington, D.C. Reprinted by permission.

To Random House, Inc., for excerpt from Brendan Gill, *Here at the New Yorker*, copyright 1975 by Random House, Inc. Reprinted by permission.

To S.C.M. Press Ltd. for excerpt from Ruth Rouse, *The World's Student Christian Federation*, copyright 1948 by S.C.M. Press Ltd. Reprinted by permission.

To the National Board of the YWCA of the U.S.A. for excerpt from Frances Helen Mains and Grace Loucks Elliott, *From Deep Roots: The Story of the YWCA's Religious Dimension*, copyright 1974 by the National Board of the YWCA of the U.S.A. Reprinted by permission.

To the National Council of Churches for excerpt from James J. Bacik, "Campus Ministry: Theological Reflections from a Catholic Perspective," in *Invitation to Dialogue: The Theology of College Chaplaincy and Campus Ministry*, ed. Robert Rue Parsonage, copyright 1986 by the National Council of Churches. Reprinted by permission.

Library of Congress Cataloging-in-Publication Data

Shockley, Donald G., 1937–
  Campus ministry.

    Bibliography: p.
    Includes index.
    1. Church work with students—United States.
2. College students—United States—Religious
life. I. Title.
BV1610.S47 1989   259'.24   88-32563
ISBN 0-8042-1583-9

© copyright The Westminster/John Knox Press 1989
10 9 8 7 6 5 4 3 2 1
Printed in the United States of America
The Westminster/John Knox Press
Louisville, Kentucky 40202

Foreword

Writing a book has one thing in common with composing a letter: what you say and how you say it depend upon the identity of your intended reader. My purpose in writing is to be an interpreter and advocate of campus ministry, the vocation I have followed for twenty-five years. The primary audience for which I have written is not campus ministers themselves since, presumably, they have no need to be convinced of the importance of what they do. Nevertheless, I have been conscious of the campus minister as one whose response to what I have said will be crucial to its effectiveness. If the book should stimulate discussion among my professional peers, it is they who are most likely to bring it to the attention of a much wider audience for whom, fundamentally, it is intended.

My chief objective in writing is to reach pastors and lay-persons in the hope of drawing them into conversation about campus ministry, its surprising history, and its great potential for the future. I also hope that this book will get into the hands of campus administrators and concerned faculty members and that it will be accessible to students. I have therefore written with the expectation that my readers will be a diverse company, bound by a common curiosity to know more about the church's ministry in higher education.

I must also say that this book is not a campus ministry primer in the sense that it can provide basic, practical information. Nor is it comprehensive in scope with respect to its treatment of history, its choice of themes for theological reflection, or its suggestion of priorities for the future. Rather, the value of this volume should be in its presentation of a veteran campus minister in the process of thinking seriously about his vocation and how it relates to the larger mission of the whole church in the whole world. I do not seek general acceptance of my point of view; I merely hope to do my part in encouraging thought and conversation on a topic which is very dear to my heart.

Anyone who writes about the early years of religious activity on American campuses will be indebted to the pioneering work of Clarence P. Shedd, and I am no exception. His *Two Centuries of Student Christian Movements* (New York: Association Press, 1934) and its sequel, *The Church Follows Its Students* (New Haven: Yale University Press, 1938), are the closest thing we have to campus ministry classics. I am also indebted to a 1948 memoir by Ruth Rouse, *The World's Student Christian Federation* (London: S.C.M. Press), which describes her long role of leadership in the organization which gave the book its title.

I wish I could personally acknowledge the contributions of all who have helped me find my way in campus ministry but, of course, I cannot do so. I think first of all of the scores of students with whom friendship has been deep and long-lasting and from whom I have learned a great deal. I think of all the colleagues and old friends in the profession itself who, though we may be many miles distant from each other, are constant companions in a very special way. In recent years the Sunday morning congregation in Cannon Chapel at Emory University has been especially important as my primary point of identification with the household of faith. Many in that community have been a constant source of encouragement, and I am very grateful to them all.

When writers of books reach this particular point in the foreword, they inevitably speak about the impact of their preoccupation with such projects upon their families. What they say is true. Without the love, understanding, and encouragement of my wife, Mary Jim, this book would not have been possible. I have been blessed during this period of writing about campus ministry to have two sons and a daughter attending Emory University, which I serve as chaplain. Together they are a source of such affection and fatherly pride that I have dedicated this work to them as a gesture of inexpressible gratitude.

Contents

To
Scott, James, and Allison Shockley

Introduction

It is said that the word for *crisis* in the Chinese language is written by combining two characters, one representing danger and the other representing opportunity. I cannot vouch for the accuracy of this saying, but it does provide an important perspective on an overworked word. Even if crisis is too trite a word for the situation of campus ministry today, it is nevertheless true that the profession is facing both danger and opportunity.

The most immediate danger for campus ministry now is the withdrawal of support by funding sources, most of which are church related, whether they be concerned individuals, local churches, or the budgets of various campus ministry boards and agencies. Simply put, the financial pie of the mainline Protestant churches is not expanding enough to accommodate the desires of all who are seeking a piece of it. Portions are getting smaller and some are being eliminated for the sake of others. Decisions are being made based upon how the importance of one program is perceived relative to another. In such an environment the programs which are less well understood are at a distinct disadvantage. Unfortunately, this is often the case where campus ministry is concerned. For example, people in the churches, and even those in the denominational boards and agencies, may feel they have a much better grasp of what church-related hospitals, children's homes, or summer camps are doing than they do of what goes on in a typical campus ministry program at a college or university.

The opportunity in this crisis situation is that it provides the chance, perhaps the necessity, for the story of campus ministry to be told. It is a very important story in the history of the church, but one which has not been told often enough or well enough. Campus ministers themselves may not know fully the legacy they have inherited; very few courses in seminaries highlight the church's ministry in higher education. Worse, the contemporary mission of campus ministry is not often described in the persuasive and compelling terms it deserves. If the story is ever going to be told in language which the churches can understand and appreciate, now is the time.

If financial exigency provides the occasion for telling the campus ministry story, it does not provide the proper motive for doing so. As long as the posture of campus ministry in relation to the church is that of a seldom-seen relative, showing up at the door yet again to ask for help, the story will not be taken seriously. What campus ministry has to say is vitally important to the welfare of the whole church. In a carefully prepared statement on campus ministry, the U.S. Conference of Catholic Bishops said:

> We bring to the attention of the whole Church the importance of campus ministry for the future well-being of the Church and society. . . . Campus ministry is an integral part of the Church's mission to the world and must be seen in that light.[1]

When campus ministers tell their story today it is not merely in order to justify an appeal for continued financial support. Rather, it is out of genuine concern for the welfare of the church and society that the story is told. Campus ministry is not a distant cousin; it is a member of the immediate family, and the status of its health therefore affects the well-being of the church as a whole.

The Church Beyond Itself

Out of the richness of his spiritual journey in a contemplative monastic order, a monk once said of us all, "We already have that which we most fervently seek." His reference was to the personal resources immediately available to every individual through disciplined prayer. While the church as a whole may not already possess all that it seeks and needs, it certainly has more going for it in terms of mission and ministry than it generally knows. I speak specifically of the witness and work of those whose field of service takes them outside the scope of traditional, family-oriented local church programs. Such ministries are almost too numerous to mention: chaplaincies in the military, in hospitals, on campuses, and in homes for the aged; inner-city ministries of various kinds, ministries in jails and prisons, and rural missions of multiple descriptions; teachers and administrators and ordained persons in a variety of secular jobs. But when the church asks itself how it is doing, these ministries are forgotten; its attention turns exclusively to the local congregations.

It is time for a much broader stock-taking by the church as a whole. It is time to ask whether the church exists in some form beyond the local church and, if it does, what this church beyond the church has to say for the good of the whole enterprise. As a veteran campus minister, I am not in a position to speak for all whose ministry takes them beyond the local church, but I do know a great deal about the church's stake in higher education and I believe that my experience in ministry in that arena has given me an important perspective on the contemporary problems of the church as a whole.

The signs are everywhere apparent that, according to customary norms, most of the mainline Protestant churches in America are in trouble. The astonishing boom in church membership growth during the 1950s peaked in the mid-sixties and membership statistics have declined every year since. Ironically, most campus ministers who are old enough remember the sixties as the golden age of the profession, a time when students cared enough about peace and justice to take major risks in their behalf. The fact that one of the most exciting eras in campus ministry coincided with the beginning of a mass exodus of young people from local church programs has left a legacy of mutual suspicion and the insistence that campus ministers be more closely identified with local congregations. But any attempt to clip the wings of campus ministry in the wake of an era of generally acknowledged excesses would be a serious mistake. The homogenization of the church and its ministries is not the solution; it is the problem. Insofar as the church has grown uncomfortable or uncertain about campus ministry, the proper response ought to be communication rather than control. Certainly, communication is a two-way street: if we want the church to care more about us, we must show that we care about it.

I write in a mood of great hopefulness about the restoration of campus ministry to the prominent role in the mission of the church which it formerly enjoyed. While the legacy of the sixties is important and still has much to teach, it is time to think about other things. It is time both to get behind that era and to get beyond it. We must look again at earlier times in order to reground ourselves in the heritage of student Christian movements whose contributions merit perpetual remembrance and celebration. But we turn our attention to the past for the sake of the future. No era of church history can be repeated, and we must resist the temptation to judge ourselves by comparison to idealized images of an earlier age. The most interesting era for campus ministry in the mission of the church may be just beginning, and the time which must capture our imagination and energy is therefore the present.

Toward a Faith That Thinks

What we do in campus ministry, and in the church generally, must be rooted in thoughtful faith and reflect the ongoing ministry of the one who laid down his life for the sake of the world. Campus ministers have some important theological work to do, and it must be offered as a gift to the whole church. When we read the Bible and reflect upon the great doctrinal affirmations of the church from the perspective of ministry in higher education, the tradition comes alive for us and speaks to us in fresh and even surprising ways.

History teaches us that when an institution—political, religious, or otherwise—becomes obsessed with the details of self-preservation, it has entered a period of decline. This is more true of the church than of any other institution, since the church was founded by one who preached self-denial and came to believe that his own life had to be abandoned for the sake of the gospel. Now is not the time for those who care about campus ministry to go into a survival mode. Now is the time for the church to determine what its mission in higher education is and to fulfill it with renewed vigor.

Historical and theological reflection, done with great sensitivity to the present situation of church and culture, and with a focus on ministry in the academic world, will push us toward confident decision making and constructive actions. It can be taken for granted that certain things are constants wherever the life of the church manifests itself: God will be praised, prayers lifted, pastoral concern for each other expressed. It would be redundant for anyone to say that these are things Christian people ought to do. With respect to the present topic therefore, much will be left unsaid when the time comes to speak concretely about what needs to be done. The approach will be to press forward an agenda of priorities which may provoke discussion and debate. If that happens and if, in the process, we are exploring theological imperatives rather than grinding political axes, the church will be the better for it.

A Preliminary Confession

I became a campus chaplain in 1964, the year when the first wave of the baby-boom generation enrolled in college, and I have been devoted to such work ever since. From 1967 to 1971, I spent, off and on, a total of about fifteen months in the San Francisco area pursuing graduate studies. From 1972 to 1979, I lived in southern California and experienced at first hand the emergence of the "Jesus freaks" and attendant phenomena. I feel a deep sense of attachment to this generation of students, most of whom have never found their place in the church even though they took the spiritual dimension of life more seriously than subsequent student generations have. I confess that I, too, have had my problems with the church. During my student days I served as a part-time rural pastor for five years. My first appointment following seminary was a two-year term as associate minister in a prosperous suburban church in the deep South during the height of the racial crisis. Well before my thirtieth birthday I had experienced the church at both ends of the economic spectrum, and I viewed it as a very human institution indeed.

I need not tell the whole story. It is sufficient to say that in my life as a minister I have struggled to resolve the ethical, intellectual, and aesthetic quarrels I have had and continue to have with the church as an all-too-human organization. But I am proud to say that, in spite of appealing opportunities to do otherwise, I have clung to my identity as a minister of the church through thick and thin. I have no fundamental doubt about where I stand in this world; my place is in the church and my life's work is to be one of its representatives in the arena of higher education. I am not a spiritual Lone Ranger. The communion of the saints, solidarity with brothers and sisters of the faith in other places and times, is as dear to my heart now as it was when I first learned to say, with the innocence of childhood, that I believed in it.

Nevertheless, serving in what I have come to understand as the church beyond the church, it has been necessary to maintain a critical distance from the mainstream of local parish life. I hope that the reasons for this will become clear in the pages which follow. Basically, it is because a campus minister daily rubs elbows with the most articulate and well-informed skeptics in the society, some of whom are nevertheless sympathetic to the church and some of whom are not. In such an environment one cannot respond by merely assuming a defensive posture in behalf of the institutional status quo. One has to listen conscientiously and to think about what the church is doing and what it might do differently. To do this one must be able to tolerate an unusual degree of vulnerability and learn how to stand one's ground gently.

I have learned in a quarter-century of chaplaincy ministry that the church exists beyond itself. And, like St. Paul way out in Corinth, I believe that I have heard, seen, and felt some realities which are inaccessible in Jerusalem, and that the time for reporting back is long past. In the hope that it is never too late, I am eager now to talk about my life in campus ministry, to be an interpreter and advocate of the work to which I have devoted so much of my life. I am motivated to write by concern for the welfare of the church as a whole and not merely for that part of it which is closest to me. Based upon what I see and hear as I move among students and faculty today, I have high hopes for the mission and ministry of the church tomorrow. That, above all else, is what moves me to write.

PART I

A Past Full of Surprises

In his history of the *New Yorker* magazine Brendan Gill wrote:

> If the unexamined life is not worth living, the unexamined past is not worth possessing; it bears fruit only by being held continuously up to the light, and it is as changeable and as full of surprises, pleasant and unpleasant, as the future.[1]

While it does not normally occur to us that the past is changeable and full of surprises, experience teaches us that this is true. Perhaps the clearest example of how the past can change and surprise us may be drawn from the process of psychotherapy. When we tell our own story to a skilled listener, one who knows how to guide us in the telling, the surprises come. Even as we retell experiences we think we understand fully, we may get in touch with aspects of our lives which we have long shielded from consciousness. New insights come and we find that we understand ourselves differently. Our past has changed.

Once we understand these dynamics, we can never again think of the past as dead. Just as our own personal memory is a storehouse of insight and information, so also our collective history is a living resource, waiting to yield its treasures in the process of retelling. Contemporary examples of this truth are abundant. It is fair to say, for example, that for many generations the history of America was told without due representation of the role of women or of ethnic minority peoples. The realization that this is so has required the retelling of the story of our past, and in a way that causes it both to surprise us and to change our understanding of how we have become who we are as a people.

Examining the past from the perspective of a particular interest has a way of both illuminating the present and suggesting alternatives for the future. The story of students in the life of the church has not been told well enough or often enough, and it is a story which needs to be heard today. Campus ministers themselves do not know this story very well, particularly those who are young in the profession. In seminaries today there is virtually no attention given to the church's ministry in higher education, whether past or present. But it is nevertheless an important strain of church history which, when it is examined and retold, has a remarkable capacity to surprise us and to rekindle our hopes for the leadership of young adults in the mission of the church.

I do not propose to examine in detail all the antecedents of what we know today as campus ministry. Perhaps the first surprise to emerge as one begins to think about such things is the discovery that the story reaches all the way back to the beginnings of higher education in America and is quite complex and abundant in detail. Were we to take into account the interaction of church and university in other lands and in earlier times, it would be a rich tale indeed. For our purposes it is enough to look at the tradition in the U.S.

Even so, our approach will be more topical than chronological and comprehensive; we will enter into dialogue with selected portions of the story, asking all along what the word of the past is to the present. We will take soundings into various periods from the beginning through the high water mark of denominational campus ministries, the decade of the 1950s. In my judgment it is not yet possible to consider anything after 1964 as campus ministry history, for we are still living in the aftermath of the unique era we call the sixties. It is impossible to understand the situation of campus ministry today without comprehending the fact that the profession has not yet recovered from the turbulent, exhilarating, and, in many ways, destructive impact of those years. We cannot go forward as we should until we unravel the tangled knot of the sixties and rediscover the loose threads which can connect us once more to our own history. But we will save that discussion until we are ready to focus on how it is we can move from where we are to where we ought to be.

It is important for us to know how the first student Christian societies in America began and what they were like. The story of the Young Men's and Young Women's Christian Associations in the development of campus ministry programs in the nineteenth and early twentieth centuries is likewise critical for understanding much about both the church and the university. The emergence of student Christian *movements* as a global phenomenon prior to the great world wars is the most astonishing aspect of the story to review. The emergence of large public universities after the Civil War and the response of denominations to that novel development are also a critical part of the story. By the time we have done all this and had a look at the distinctive contribution of church-related schools, and of black colleges in particular, we will have an impressive list of things which, for most of us, will have the character of surprise.

1

Campus Ministries Begun by Students

In one of his classic studies of the early days of campus religious programs, Clarence Shedd remarked that there were two basic approaches to be found. The first can be described as student-centered church work, and the second as church-centered student work.[1] In the former case the needs of students are what motivate the church's presence, in whatever form, in higher education. In the latter case the needs of the church, whether they are to keep students in the fold or to recruit and train its future leaders, are the primary motivating factors. The distinction remains a useful benchmark when we want to measure and define what we are about in campus ministry.

In the beginning, student Christians took the initiative in developing programs which were designed to serve their own spiritual needs when they determined that institutional responses in such matters were inadequate. Interestingly, it was a long time before the churches themselves developed formal programs of outreach to students, and their motivation was at least partially to keep students from leaving the fold under the influence of alien philosophies.

This is not to suggest that the desire to keep students in the fellowship of the church is somehow suspect, or to imply that the motivations of students and of the church to initiate student programs are antithetical. After all, it was the church which established colleges in the first place and sought, through them, to serve the students' desire for knowledge as well as to provide itself with educated leadership. Nevertheless, as we shall shortly see, students from the beginning felt a need for more in the way of religious nurture than the formal efforts of church and college were providing. And that is where our story begins.

The Student Christian Societies

In a sermon at the funeral of a young schoolmaster, Cotton Mather told how the deceased had joined with a few other students to create a Christian society at Harvard in 1706.[2] While this is the earliest existing reference to a student Christian organization in America, it is reasonable to suppose that there were others like it. It would be safe to assume that students began to organize themselves into religious societies soon after the first American campuses appeared. The interesting thing here is that students began to organize their own religious societies despite the fact that the first colleges themselves were founded by church bodies in the interest of providing resources to educate the clergy. The ethos of colonial colleges must have been saturated with religion. Nevertheless, students wanted to gather with their peers for the sake of mutual support and common study. The additional fact that these early organizations were secret societies suggests that the students felt their meetings might not win the approval of either the college authorities or the local clergy.

Membership in these early student societies was by invitation only, and a covenant was entered into which anticipated that one's behavior would be monitored by the other members. The level of discipline expected was such that participants would not hesitate to expel from the group any member who violated certain norms and remained unrepentant. It is intriguing to remember that, during this time period, John and Charles Wesley organized their Holy Club across the Atlantic at Oxford University, a group which was apparently quite similar in nature to those at Harvard and, we assume, elsewhere. In the colonial period the student Christian societies were of two varieties. One was devotional in character and concentrated upon prayer, Bible study, and mutual support in living a devout life. The other type of society was more intellectual in character and devoted itself to theological discussion and debate.[3]

The significance of these groups comes into sharper focus when we remember an important fact. When we talk about religion in early America, most of us tend to assume that nearly everyone then was a loyal church member. Stereotypical views of Puritan control of the Massachusetts Bay Colony present the colonists as uniformly devout folks. The reality was very much to the contrary. By 1800 the churches could count as adherents only fourteen percent of the population, and more than a hundred years would have to pass before the figure would exceed fifty percent.[4] At times, such as immediately after the Revolutionary War when atheism and materialist philosophies were popular, there was a great deal of hostility toward religion. In the Dartmouth graduating class of 1799, there was only one student who was known to be a confessing Christian.[5] There is no reason to believe that Dartmouth was exceptional in this respect. It is important to understand that the social context of the early student Christian organizations was not as sympathetic as we might often assume.

But the role of religion in American history has been dynamic, to say the least. When that young Christian walked across the stage at Dartmouth to receive his diploma, he was headed into a society which was about to enter a century of revivalism and missionary fervor. The disestablishment of religion, which the constitution of the new nation took pains to ensure, would by no means hurt the churches. The church as a truly voluntary association, energized by revivalism, was destined for power and influence of the most compelling sort—that which is brought by growing popular acceptance. On the campuses a new version of the student Christian society would play an important role in shaping the church's understanding of its mission.

The most famous episode in the history of student Christian societies in the U.S. was the "haystack prayer meeting" which occurred at Williams College in 1806. Five students, led by Samuel Mills, the devout son of a minister, went into a meadow near the college to pray. The rise of a sudden thunderstorm caused them to seek shelter by a haystack where they continued to talk and pray. Mills spoke with urgency about the obligation of Christians to persons in foreign lands and suggested to his friends that their prayers were empty unless they were themselves willing to be missionaries should God call them to serve in such a capacity. Four of the students made the commitment on the spot, and all agreed to continue their meetings and to persuade others to join them. At this time the original societies, based upon devotion or theological discussion, were joined by a third type, the student missionary society.

When Mills and a core of friends moved on to Andover Seminary, they formed a student missionary society which in the sixty-four years of its existence saw two hundred and fifty of its members leave for service overseas.[6] But the original group felt their chances of being sponsored by churches in America were minimal, since there were no boards of foreign mission at that point, and the students perceived the churches to be indifferent, if not hostile, to their vision. They were surprised when the General Association of Congregational Churches of Massachusetts responded favorably to their petition and created the first American missionary-sending society. Although Mills was not among them, the first five missionaries were dispatched to India in 1812. We need to remind ourselves that boarding a wooden sailing vessel and heading out to sea carried considerably more risk than spending several hours on a modern jet airplane. Returning from an exploratory trip to Africa, young Mills himself became ill, died, and was buried at sea. He never had the opportunity to establish himself as a missionary.

The passion of students to spread the gospel around the world did not reach full flower until much later in the nineteenth century. Since those early days, students have continued to make a significant difference in the life of the church. When they gather to pray, discuss theological issues, or talk about the mission of the church, there is enormous potential among them. Much depends upon how attentive the leadership of the church is to the vision and courage of those who have not yet learned which things are impossible. It is easy to debunk this original missionary impulse as the misguided zeal of American imperialism, and thereby to devalue the vision and hope which motivated student Christians in the nineteenth century. While it is certainly true that the people and resources of other lands have been exploited by Western, Christian nations, it is also true that those who scatter the seeds of the gospel, however pure or impure their motives, cannot forever control the harvest which will follow. The vitality of the church in the Third World today is a phenomenon which is not unrelated to the missionary enterprise of earlier generations, regardless of how one chooses to evaluate the contribution of people like Samuel Mills.

The Student Christian Associations

In 1844 twelve young clerks in a London dry-goods establishment came together to find some way of relating the Christian faith to their experience in the everyday world of work in the environment of a major city. They decided to call their group a "Young Men's Christian Association" (YMCA), and very soon the idea was adopted by persons similarly situated in other cities in Great Britain. A letter about these associations, written by an American student studying in Edinburgh, may have led to the founding of the first YMCA in the U.S., in Boston in 1851. It is important for modern readers to dismiss from their minds the contemporary image of the "Y" as a physical fitness salon or agency for the propagation of summer camps. In its origin the YMCA was very much an evangelical Christian outreach to young men working in cities. The famous evangelist Dwight L. Moody got his start as director of the YMCA of Chicago, where he first began to hone his skill as a preacher. It is still more important to note the genesis of the "Y" as a ministry concerned with *vocation*, with the weekday world of young men.

For reasons which I do not believe are entirely clear to

anyone, chapters of the YMCA were formed both at the University of Michigan and at the University of Virginia in 1858. In less than twenty years associations were started on more than forty campuses in the U.S. even though there was no apparent, organized developmental effort under way. In fact, leaders of the city-based movement, which was also growing rapidly, were puzzled by what was happening on the campuses. Was it the name alone which stimulated imaginations and triggered a new approach to Christian presence on the campuses? I think there was a more significant affinity between the two phenomena: the campus "Y's" were born in the environment of the large public institutions of higher education. Just as the young clerks in London were concerned about the implications of city life for their faith (and vice versa), the students were experiencing the new phenomenon of the nonchurch-related university and therefore had similar concerns.

This is one of the most significant periods in the history of campus ministry. As we have seen, the early student Christian societies were concerned primarily for the nurture of individuals through devotional activities, the provision of opportunities for theological discussion, and the encouragement of the missionary enterprise. With the coming of the YMCA to campus, we see a new emphasis upon the "carrying of religion into the sphere of the daily occupation."[7] A more comprehensive understanding of the role of faith in the learning environment begins to emerge. Community service projects, for example, were part of the "Y" program at the University of Virginia from the beginning. The sponsorship of public lectures by distinguished Christian leaders was also introduced by the campus YMCAs. At this early stage one can see the outlines of contemporary forms of campus ministry which embrace a broad range of programs and activities.

Although women students had participated in the campus YMCAs from the beginning, the eventual affiliation of the campus "Y's" with the larger city-based organization of the same name would turn their involvement into a controversial issue. At the University of Michigan, for example, the campus YMCA, which had advocated the admission of women students to the university, changed its name to the "Student Christian Association" (SCA) in anticipation of the enrollment of women in 1870. But the Michigan SCA continued its affiliation with the national YMCA and sent delegations including women students to its intercollegiate gatherings. Under pressure from national staff, the Michigan students refused to divide into gender-specific associations, holding out until 1895, when the YWCA was such a strong national movement that the Michigan women wanted their own local chapter.[8]

Actually, a "Young Women's Christian Association" (YWCA) had been formed in London as a parallel organization to the original group, and it was only a matter of time until the YWCA would also appear on campuses in this country.[9] The first campus YWCA was formed at the Illinois State Normal University in 1873, and by 1889 there were chapters on 142 campuses. The YMCA had likewise spread at an astonishing rate, with units on 181 campuses by 1885. We will have more to say about how and why the "Y" so captured the minds and hearts of Christian students in the late nineteenth century. At this point, several important observations can already be made. As the campus "Y" became institutionalized, the professional leadership which emerged was composed of persons who were not ordained ministers; throughout their histories, the YMCA and the YWCA have been ecumenically organized movements led by laypersons.

The SCAs were forerunners not only of campus ministry but also of the student affairs programs of contemporary universities. The buildings which were constructed, many of them very impressive in scale, likewise anticipated not just the denominational houses but also student union structures which the universities themselves would later erect and operate. The University of Michigan is the most important case study of how the SCAs both moved to meet the spiritual needs of students and offered a comprehensive response to their general welfare. Orientation activities for freshmen, a handbook for new students, an employment bureau, listings of available housing options, a student directory, used book exchange, clubs and language classes for international students, and volunteer community service programs all were initiated by the SCA at Michigan. And these were by no means simply nominal efforts. The employment bureau, for example, existed for thirty-five years and made 2,400 job placements in the academic year 1919–20.[10]

While these are the kinds of programs and statistics which warm the hearts of those who pay the bills for campus ministry today, we must remind ourselves that the impact made by SCAs on the lives of individual students cannot be captured by numbers. How could we measure the long-range impact of campus YWCAs in which

> prayer groups had helped women to find their tongues for the first time as Christian women, to formulate in their own words their needs and hopes, to express them to one another. Participation in group meetings helped them to develop their capacity and willingness to speak in public. Sharing with one another their personal experience of God gave them courage.[11]

The story of the SCAs is a proud and wonderful chapter in the history of campus ministry and of the work of the church in the world.

The Student Christian Movements

To pick up a critically important aspect of the campus ministry story, we must step back a bit in order to see what happened when the movement to create campus Christian associations met the rejuvenated spirit of missionary zeal which we saw first in Samuel Mills and his friends. First of all, it is important to relate how the YMCA itself became a national, then an international, movement.

The Philadelphian Society was a student Christian organization founded at Princeton University in 1825. Still strong in the academic year 1875–76, it became the center of a significant religious awakening on the campus. In the midst of the excitement Dwight L. Moody was persuaded to make an appearance, his first visit to preach on an American campus. The enthusiasm created by the Princeton revival was such that the students decided to send out teams to other campuses to tell the story of what had happened. This is the beginning of the first intercollegiate student Christian movement in America.[12] But there is a great deal more to the story.

One cold December night in 1876, Princeton student Luther Wishard found that he had insufficient coal for the fireplace in his room and went upstairs to borrow some from a couple of students whom he did not know very well. William E. Dodge, father of the two students and a member of the International Committee of the YMCA, was in their room for a visit. The four of them began to talk about the religious awakening at Princeton and the students' continuing desire to spread the enthusiasm to other campuses. Dodge told them about a forthcoming YMCA convention to be held in Louisville, Kentucky, and suggested that they consider attempting to gather their own student conference in conjunction with that meeting. As a result of subsequent efforts by the Philadelphian Society, student delegates from twenty-five campuses in as many states came to Louisville where they held an independent conference. When the meetings concluded, the Intercollegiate YMCA movement had been formally established with Luther Wishard as its corresponding secretary.[13] As we have seen, the campus "Y" movement spread very rapidly in the U.S.

It is fascinating to review how several streams of student activity and interest came together in the late nineteenth century to create an unprecedented explosion of student participation in the mission of the church. As in the case of the earlier haystack prayer meeting, it is possible to pinpoint the catalytic episode which made the "Y" movement go international and create a student Christian movement of global proportions. As a result of a long revival crusade in Great Britain, during which he was invited to preach at the great universities in Oxford, Cambridge, and Edinburgh, Dwight L. Moody's interest in students grew, as did his confidence in his ability to reach them. After first considering a month-long summer Bible conference for local YMCA secretaries, he and Luther Wishard decided to have such a conference, led by the evangelist, for students instead of their adult leaders. Some 250–300 young men gathered in Mt. Hermon,

Massachusetts, in 1886 at the site of a school for boys which Moody had established. The principal objective which was achieved, and which made the meeting historically significant, was not one that the conference leadership had in mind.

Grace Wilder and her brother Robert, children of missionary parents, were both students—he at Princeton and she at Mt. Holyoke College. Both had been praying for a surge of student interest in foreign missions and, on their respective campuses, had begun to challenge other students to sign a simple pledge which said, "We, the undersigned, declare ourselves willing and desirous, God permitting, to go to the unevangelized portions of the world."[14] When Robert was persuaded to attend the Mt. Hermon conference, he came with the intention of getting as many conferees as possible to sign the pledge. On the last night, the number of students at the conference who had signed the pledge reached one hundred! And, of course, there was great enthusiasm to spread the word from campus to campus, recruiting ever more signers.

As the missionary fervor mushroomed, fears were raised that the YMCA and YWCA movements would be so overwhelmed by this one interest that their original purposes, still very important, would get lost. A summit conference of interested parties was held and a decision made to create a separate but closely related organization to be called, appropriately enough, the Student Volunteer Movement for Foreign Missions. John R. Mott, a Cornell University student who had had his arm twisted to get him to attend the Mt. Hermon conference, was persuaded to become college secretary of the YMCA and to assume specific responsibility for organizing the Student Volunteer Movement. Mott kept the assignment for the next thirty years, and during the course of its history the movement saw more than 11,000 students actually go overseas as missionaries.[15] With Mott's help on the homefront, Luther Wishard and his spouse, inspired by the vision of a YMCA in every college founded on the mission field, left for a journey lasting almost four years. They visited Japan, Turkey, Syria, India, Ceylon, China, Malaya, Siam, Burma, Egypt, Greece, Bulgaria, and

Bohemia. Everywhere they went, they established or strength-
ened existing student Christian organizations under the umbrella
of the YMCA. In similar fashion, the YWCA also became international in scope and spread rapidly in many countries.

This history is so rich that it is impossible to follow it
straight through or even to mention many aspects of it which are
quite important. I must simply assert that the leadership development aspect of the movements, at home and abroad, played an
indispensable role in raising up persons of vision and courage,
both in the churches and in the emerging nations. John R. Mott
himself played an essential role in preparing the ground for the
modern ecumenical movement. For these early leaders of what
we now call campus ministry, the only way truly to experience
the church of Jesus Christ was to realize its global dimensions to
the greatest extent possible.

It was through Mott's imagination and initiative that representatives of several national student Christian movements in
Europe and America met in Sweden to form the World Student
Christian Federation (WSCF) in 1895. He took on the additional
responsibility of General Secretary for the new organization and
promptly left for twenty months of traveling in Europe and
Asia.[16] National movements and the federation itself grew
rapidly in the years which followed, and great international
conferences were held to bring together representatives of student Christian movements from around the world. When the
World Council of Churches was formed, many of its leaders
were veterans of student Christian movements in their own
homelands.

Women were admitted as full members of the WSCF in
1905, and Ruth Rouse was appointed as secretary for the development of women's movements related to the organization. For
many years thereafter her leadership was equal to that of Mott,
and her job was, perhaps, a great deal harder because she traveled
in societies where women were just beginning to be admitted to
universities and where there was general hostility to the Christian faith. She organized student gatherings in Russia in the years
just before the revolution, when the czarist government was

especially anxious to prevent the formation of student groups. In other countries she would visit campuses reputed to have only one woman who professed to be a Christian and leave behind her a new Christian society of women. Her story is an uncommon narrative of courage and vision, and it shows more clearly than any other the contributions of women in the early days of campus ministry.[17]

I believe that World War I marks the end of this major phase of student movement development. While work continued in Asia and elsewhere, the phenomenon of students in Europe, and later from the U.S., fighting and killing each other at the behest of their governments forever changed the student Christian world. While the student movements played an important role in relief efforts, and while there were many examples of extraordinary understanding and sympathy which transcended enemy lines, a new maturity about evangelism and mission was necessary. That the lives of persons are decisively affected by *systems*—racism, war, economic injustice—became an inescapable reality. Therefore, goodwill and service projects were not enough; there had to be a larger Christian point of view on life as a whole. It was necessary that the student movement be "intellectually more competent" and begin to question the role of the educational enterprise itself.[18]

The era of the development of a worldwide student Christian movement was one of the great periods in the history of the church. This is not to say that the era is entirely over. The WSCF still exists, with member movements in many countries. Some of the national student movements are very active in liberation struggles in their homelands, and regional coordinators maintain a network of communication on a global basis. But there is no national ecumenical student Christian movement in the U.S. today which is linked to the WSCF. Efforts are under way to rebuild both denominational and ecumenical movements through regional and national conferences, but it is too early to know what the outcome will be.

2

Campus Ministries Begun by the Churches

When one begins to think historically about the engagement of Christian faith and higher education, it quickly becomes apparent that there are many angles to the story. Although our desire is not to be comprehensive but to be selective in our survey, it is important for us to consider the contributions which colleges and universities related to the church have themselves made to what, in the broadest sense of the term, one would call campus ministry. While we must speak in the most general way, it is important to acknowledge that the church is the mother of higher education in America and through its related institutions continues to play an important, if less certain, role in it. The evolution of the distinctive role of the college chaplain in such institutions is likewise a significant part of the overall story of campus ministry.

Even though our reference to the role of church-related colleges and universities will necessarily be brief, the singular contributions of institutions which have historically served a predominantly black constituency help us to understand more clearly what Christian higher education is. It is likewise important for us to note, however briefly, the beginning of women's participation in higher education, an opportunity which was originally denied them in a society dominated by white Protestant males. Although we may rightfully lament the slow pace of change toward equality and justice in the nation, a backward look of a hundred years provides another perspective. Ours is a society in which the status of women has changed significantly in a relatively short period of time, and the momentum of the movement is such that more change is in prospect.

Because of the challenge which campus ministry faces at the present time, it will be most instructive for us to have a closer look at how the churches responded to the emergence of large public universities following the Civil War. Although these schools were typically little different from their church-related counterparts in the beginning, it was correctly surmised that they were destined to be "secular" places in which religion would play an ever-decreasing role at the official level. For a variety of reasons, the handwriting was on the wall: a majority of students in the future would be attending secular institutions and the church's use of higher education to influence the nature of the society would be sharply limited. New approaches and a new vision would be essential.

As we have seen, it was the SCAs which took the initiative in responding to the changing ethos of the universities, and they played a very influential role for many years. But to a great extent the associations were dependent upon a continuing evangelical Protestant consensus in the state universities to maintain their central role. In the twentieth century, as decades of immigration began to make an impact and Roman Catholic and Jewish students enrolled in greater numbers, and as the denominations became more guarded in their relations with each other, religious pluralism began to set the tone of campus life, and the era of denomination-based campus ministries began.

Church-related Higher Education

One cannot read very much in the history of higher education without coming across a quotation from the founding documents of Harvard College, which shows that the motivation for its founding had to do with the colonists' desire for an educated clergy. But we must remember that in that time and place the distinction between the religious and secular spheres was not sharply drawn; the Bible was the primary document of civil governance and clergy were its chief interpreters. To say that Harvard was founded to provide an educated clergy had a larger meaning than one would infer from a statement today concerning the establishment of a new theological seminary. In founding the first institution of higher education in what was to become the United States of America, the colonists were acting on their hope of creating an exemplary society, a new order in which the intention of God for human life would prevail.

To assume that the churches established colleges only in order to meet their own internal needs for leadership would be to miss a very important point, not only about the past but also about the future. The church founded colleges because of its paramount concern for the general welfare of the society. Their mission was to train what might be thought of as morally intelligent leadership for the whole community, not just for the church. As a democratic form of national government emerged, it became all the more critical to be concerned about what the people in general valued. Without an educated citizenry, democracy would ultimately fail. At the time, it seemed rather clear that familiarity with a distinct body of literature drawn from the classics, the Bible, Christian theology, and moral philosophy would meet the aims of education. All of this, of course, was to take place in an ethos of Protestant piety.

The schools founded by the churches were to a very important degree more *public* in character than many of the state-sponsored institutions which were to come later.[1] That is to say, their purpose was to train leaders for the society rather than to teach specific vocational skills as the great land-grant universities were founded specifically to do. It is also important to remember that church-founded schools dominated American higher education until the dawn of the twentieth century. At the time of the Civil War, 175 of the 182 colleges and universities in the nation were church related.[2] The provision of education, and not just education on religious topics, was understood to be an essential form of the church's ministry in society, and that is why even a casual survey of the origins of campus ministry must consider the existence of the colleges themselves, quite apart from any specialized forms of ministry within them.

In the beginning, college presidents were almost invariably clergymen. Even the early tax-supported institutions, such as the Universities of Michigan and Georgia, were first headed by men of the cloth. That students would study the Scriptures, be regular participants in worship, behave as gentlemen, and be taught by devout faculty was taken for granted. Presiding at regular, perhaps daily, convocations of the whole college, the president of the church-founded schools played the role of both spiritual and academic leader, setting the tone of campus life. As we have seen, some students were not satisfied with this official religious ethos and secretly held their own meetings. No doubt there were others who did not care for either ethos.

We will have more to say about college and university chaplaincy in later chapters, but it is important to note its beginnings in the context of this brief sketch on church-related campuses. Although the Reverend Naphtali Daggett was appointed chaplain at Yale in 1755, he never had a peer to talk to; it would be more than a century before another college made such an appointment.[3] Indeed, by 1900 there were only a dozen or so college and university chaplains in the nation. The major growth in campus chaplaincy occurred following World War II, with around three hundred such positions existing in the 1950s. Interestingly, about half of these were in institutions which considered themselves independent of the church.[4]

The chaplaincy came into existence as college presidents were less able or less willing to play the role of spiritual leader for the campus community. More laypersons were appointed to presidencies, the job became more complex and demanding, faculty and student bodies became more diverse. For a variety of reasons, it was felt that another office was needed to attend to the religious dimensions of life on the campus. Although the title varied from place to place, there emerged in the private colleges and universities the unique role of the chaplain. Typically reporting directly to the president, the chaplain inherited the role of spiritual leader just as the traditions supporting the role, such as required chapel attendance, began to be abandoned. Nevertheless, voluntary chapel programs which maintain the tradition of campus-oriented worship have not only survived but in many places have continued to be quite prominent features of campus life. The basic point here is merely to take note of the emergence of a form of campus ministry which is distinct in nature and function from the denomination-based campus ministries which arose to serve the public institutions.

It is important to remember, when we long for the good old days when church-related colleges really had the atmosphere of churches, that such a thing was possible largely because everyone associated with the enterprise shared a great deal in common. In the state-sponsored universities as well, higher education was the province of white Protestant males. But so were government, business, and all other major institutions of the society. The basic commitment of the colleges to serve the national interest meant that their constituencies would change as the times changed. Furthermore, the health of the academic enterprise itself requires openness to human diversity. Both the church's commitment to service and the academy's need for openness would lead to the breakdown of the Protestant consensus, but this would occur in some places much sooner than others.

The first college opened specifically for the education of women was Georgia Female College in 1830, still alive and well as Wesleyan College in Macon, Georgia. Oberlin College came soon after, but most would not come until after the Civil War. The motivation for the higher education of women was to train them as teachers for the emerging elementary school systems, since it was felt that this task fell within the primary role thought to be appropriate for them, the nurture of children. This would be followed by the creation of a new discipline suitable for women to study, "home economics." However bad this may sound to our ears today, it is nevertheless the case that when this breakthrough came it was the result of devout folks who took risks for the sake of social change. Getting the doors open was the key; after gaining access to college, women would continually press beyond the limits imposed by traditional expectations. They would become college professors, missionary physicians, and the pioneers of "social work" in behalf of the poor.[5]

Eventually, women were admitted to colleges and universities operated for males and, finally, to all the academic options available within them, although this process of opening up continues until the present day. A similar course was followed with respect to black people: colleges exclusively for them, then the long, slow process, still going on, of equal access to the whole world of academia. It is not necessary for us to document the inclusion of Roman Catholics, Jews, and other religious and ethnic minorities in order to make the point at issue here. Because of the nature of their mission, church-related colleges and universities were destined to become pluralistic places and, just as surely, these changes would bring accommodations in the interest of hospitality. And those changes would begin to raise questions about what makes a school Presbyterian, Baptist, or whatever. Such questions take us far beyond our task here, but some consideration of the black colleges may suggest a direction for the renewal of the original vision of church-related higher education.

The Exemplary Role of the Black Colleges

Slightly more than a hundred years ago there was little educational opportunity at any level for black people in the U.S. This does not mean that there were absolutely no black people who were educated; some had acquired learning through a variety of means and some had even achieved scholarly distinction. A few schools had been established in the North by missionaries, but the great majority of black people lived in the South, where there was no formal educational opportunity to be found. After the Civil War, the federal government, churches, and philanthropic organizations rushed in to create some two hundred colleges in response to the great hunger for education which was present.[6] All of this was done without a systematic plan to allocate available resources in terms of strategic locations or types of educational programs to be made available. And, obviously, such colleges had first of all to offer programs at the elementary and secondary school levels in order to prepare students to do college work.

While we cannot tell the whole story here, we can say that in a relatively short period of time some distinctive institutions of higher education emerged. One thinks of Howard University in Washington, D.C., Fisk University in Nashville, and Morehouse and Spelman Colleges in Atlanta as examples. But most did not fare so well; they did not have the resources to do so. Through the years, many surveys have concluded that most of these colleges were never able to match their white counterparts in terms of the usual criteria of academic quality, e.g., library and laboratory resources, endowment funds, faculty research, standardized test scores, etc. But these are not the only relevant criteria for judging a college, particularly a church-related one which has a distinctive mission.

When measured in terms of service to the community and in terms of character and leadership development, the collective achievements of these colleges have been admirable indeed. In his autobiography James Farmer describes in detail his experience as a student at Wiley College, a small black campus in Texas, during the late 1930s. He speaks movingly of the influence of a professor of philosophy who took a keen personal interest, particularly in those students who showed unusual promise, and pushed them to stretch their minds and expand the horizon of their hopes. He writes of the leadership opportunities on the campus which were critical to his personal development. Farmer went on to become one of the half-dozen most influential leaders of the civil rights movement which changed the face of American society.[7]

How is one to measure the importance of the small church-related college which has a strong sense of its distinctive mission, or the contribution of dedicated teachers, forever unknown to the world at large, whose presence, in and out of the classroom, made the difference in a young person's sense of self-worth and promise? I believe that the black colleges, precisely because they have had to do so much with so little, have remained closer to the mission of Christian higher education than most of the majority-white institutions. They have also been spared the degree of pluralism with which others have had to deal because of their distinctive mission in behalf of black people.

Service has been and remains an authentic motto for the black colleges. As we have seen, that is what church-related higher education was about in the first place and, however it is defined, is what must be recovered in a meaningful way as the central motivation for church-related higher education today. It will never be enough to present such colleges as playing a conserving role in behalf of the denominations which founded them, regardless of how politically expedient such argument may be. And it will never be enough merely to point to such institutions' achievements as measured by the criteria of excellence prized by the academic world. No less than campus ministry itself, the colleges and universities related to the Christian tradition have an obligation to understand their goals in the light of the church's mission in the world.

There is no doubt about the fact that the black colleges produced the leaders who helped the nation deal with the quest for racial equality through the civil rights movement. Nevertheless, the great majority of black students who attend college today elect to enroll in white-majority institutions, apparently because of their belief that such schools will provide a superior education. But a recent study suggests that this may not be the case, at least not to the degree generally assumed. The supportive community life, larger friendship network, greater opportunities for social participation, and the greater sense of academic success and progress which black institutions offer to black students, will in many cases more than compensate for stronger academic programs to be found elsewhere. Most surprising is the observation that black colleges may be critical to the process of racial integration through their greater ability to instill the confidence and the skills necessary to function successfully in the larger society.[8]

It is time for the churches and the colleges and universities related to them to reassess what their historic connection means. There is as much confusion over what it means today to be a church-related college as there is over the question of the goals of campus ministry. The two issues are definitely related, since both have to do with the mission of the church in relation to higher education. Perhaps our discussion in the following pages concerning the future of campus ministry will be suggestive for an overall view of the church's mission in higher education, including the colleges it founded and with which it has a continuing formal relation of some kind.

The Denominational Foundations

Although Thomas Jefferson founded the University of Virginia in 1819 as a public university, the idea that the government should provide a system of higher education came rather late into general acceptance in the U.S. The Morrill Land Grant Act in 1862 provided for substantial grants of land and, later, money to the individual states for the establishment of public institutions, primarily in the fields of agriculture and mechanical arts.[9] This was a major turning point for American higher education since it not only provided federal government support of universities but also established a trend toward the equality of practical studies with the liberal arts. That there would be a nationwide network of universities, which the churches did not create and which offered curricula that departed from the traditional understanding of the nature and purpose of higher education, was a major challenge to the Protestant vision of America's future.

Having had a virtual monopoly on higher education for over two hundred years, the churches in general did not look kindly upon this development. Churches also offered resistance when public campuses began to attract significant numbers of students and when concerned persons began to broach the idea of denominational sponsorship of ministries in their behalf. The chief argument against the idea of special ministries at public institutions was that such a move would seem to sanction the existence of secular universities and undermine the church's argument that they would inevitably become godless environments. The churches wanted the students to attend church colleges on the ground that religious influence would be lacking at public institutions. The existence of campus ministries would militate against this argument in regard to state campuses. Here again, as we have seen, students took matters into their own hands and began to develop the YMCA and YWCA organizations to meet their needs. Ironically, the "secular" institutions enthusiastically welcomed the student religious organizations. Fortunately, there were prophetic souls in the church who saw the need and began to take the steps necessary to establish denominationally supported campus ministries. Politically, this meant going head to head with the presidents of church-related colleges in competition for funds, a rivalry which was destined to continue.[10]

The Unitarians were perhaps the first to develop a denominational strategy for campus ministry. Their plan was to establish churches in college towns, whose mission would be to develop significant work with students. The first was begun in Ann Arbor in 1865, and by the turn of the century the young people's society of that local church had a membership of over two hundred even though there were no more than twenty-five Unitarian students enrolled in the University of Michigan at the time.[11] Presbyterians, Episcopalians, Methodists and Roman Catholics all had campus programs of some kind at Michigan before 1890. The first Newman Club, as the Roman Catholic student organizations were called for many years, was begun at the University of Pennsylvania in 1894.[12]

It is interesting to note that by 1891, the Presbyterians had not one but two buildings at the University of Michigan, "containing a library with over ten thousand volumes, a gymnasium (the only one on the campus), a bowling alley, kitchen equipment, club rooms and an auditorium seating 350."[13] Unfortunately, this proved to be too much too soon; unable to maintain such facilities, the Presbyterians leased them to the YMCA within a few years. Nevertheless, the description of the buildings tells us much about the aspirations of both the "Y's" and the denominational programs which followed them to the public campuses. And it calls our attention again to the way in which campus ministry anticipated the needs of students and acted to meet them in numerous ways which the universities themselves would soon emulate.

The first Wesley Foundation was established in 1913 under the imaginative leadership of James C. Baker at the University of Illinois. Its stated purposes were to provide for worship, religious education, leadership development for the church, and recruitment for Christian vocations, as well as to provide "a home away from home." By the 1930s, this "foundation" pattern became more or less standard for campus ministry, with many of the campus organizations actually adopting the word, e.g., the Hillel Foundation, Westminster Foundation.[14] In more recent times the notion of a campus ministry center as a home away from home has been subject to considerable ridicule, and Christian nurture has often been dismissed as "hand-holding" which is inappropriate for mature young men and women. But behind every stereotype there is usually something worth looking for, and that is the case here.

If we remember that higher education was already undergoing a series of profound changes by the turn of the century and that the new environment of the universities was unfamiliar to most families, we will have more sympathy for what the denominational programs were attempting to do. The provision of a *place* to go where one would find a congenial environment was itself a significant ministry. In many places, the campus minister and his family actually lived in the foundation building and were continually providing hospitality for students. Needless to say, this was in the days before the two-career marriage was commonplace. The community center provides a better image of this model of campus ministry than does the home; it was and is the focus of a great variety of programs and activities.

Basically, the denominational programs paralleled the activity of the Christian associations, the main difference being that they were designed for students of one denominational group and therefore promoted the special interests of a particular tradition. Participation in local churches was emphasized and in some cases, including the first Wesley Foundation, the campus work was itself based in a local congregation. It would be more precise to say that Trinity Methodist Church, located adjacent to the campus, *became* the Wesley Foundation at the Urbana campus. In other places as well there were, and are, local congregations whose mission is campus ministry. This is a very different phenomenon from that of the near-campus church which sees itself as serving a university constituency but operates without a missional understanding to match its aspirations.

For a variety of reasons, the Christian associations began to fade while the denominational programs flowered as midcentury approached. The trend was toward an ordained professional staff, but the church-based ministries followed the "Y" pattern in developing their own national agencies, staff, literature, and denominational student movements. Beginning in the thirties and continuing into the sixties, regional and national student conferences played a prominent role in the development of this new approach to campus ministry, just as they had during the peak years of the Christian associations. The denominations got their programs established in time to ride the crest of a massive wave of expansion in higher education following World War II. In 1938, there were around two hundred full-time professional campus ministers in this country. Fifteen years later, there were one thousand, and that figure doubled to roughly two thousand by 1963.[15]

Another nineteenth-century development in denominationally supported campus ministry stands out as distinctive. The Disciples of Christ, concerned that students in public institutions would not receive instruction in religion commensurate with what they would learn in classes devoted to other disciplines, came up with the novel idea of the "Bible Chair." The church would establish a teaching program at or near a university campus, which would make high quality religious instruction available to students generally, not just to those of its own denomination. It was clearly seen that pastoral dimensions of such a role would follow in course. The first Bible chair was established at the University of Michigan in 1893, and many others were begun over a period of years.[16] On some campuses hundreds of students attended lectures on the Bible, and in some places arrangements were made to allow them to receive academic credit for courses taught under the auspices of this program. The Bible chair movement had its day. While vestiges of it remain here and there, the Disciples fell into line with the dominant form of campus ministry as variations of the foundation model emerged.

Here, as elsewhere, we are giving a very truncated version of a longer and much more complex story. But we know enough already to identify the dynamic sources of the contemporary phenomenon called campus ministry. (Although I have used the term *campus ministry* from the beginning of this discussion, the term did not gain general acceptance until the early 1950s, when it was established that the church's ministry in higher education was, or should be, more comprehensive than *student work* implied. Administrators and staff members were not to be excluded from the church's ministry in higher education.)[17] We will turn our attention now to drawing out some of the distinctive features in the heritage of the profession.

3

An Extraordinary Heritage

We began our discussion with a quotation from Brendan Gill in which he said that when the past is held up to the light it will bear fruit in ways which surprise us. While what surprises one person may not surprise another, we have seen enough of the heritage of campus ministry in the mission of the church to conclude that its contributions far exceed that for which it is normally given credit. The story simply has not been told often enough or well enough. If, after almost twenty-five years in campus ministry, the story still has the capacity to surprise and inspire me, that is reason enough for me to assume that much of what we have recounted here is fresh news to many in the life of the church.

Campus ministers today often feel that they have no solid place to stand either in the university or in the church. This sense of marginal existence is a constant theme of our meetings, with some lamenting it and others finding in it great virtue and promise. Whether one sees the margin as the border of irrelevance or the cutting edge, there is no reason for a campus minister to live with a perpetual crisis of professional identity. We are not in a profession which has no history; we need only to remind ourselves that campus ministry was not born yesterday, and it will not be gone tomorrow. The perspective of continuity through time, in the face of many changes, is helpful to us and needs to be nurtured continually.

When Jesus walked about proclaiming the kingdom of God he was often challenged to prove that anything worthy of the reference was happening in his ministry. Sometimes he pointed to miraculous events as evidence, but at other times he seemed to acknowledge that the credibility of his claims was a problem for many. At such times he told parables which portrayed mighty conclusions issuing from small beginnings, somehow coming to full realization by a process which cannot be observed. In the parable of the patient farmer, for example, Jesus pointed out that one cannot literally see the grain grow, but experience teaches that the harvest will come as a consequence of sowing the seeds (Mark 4:26–29). When we look at history rather than the present moment, we can observe both the planting and the harvest which followed and thereby learn how to be more patient with ourselves. Sometimes we have miracles to point to, and sometimes we have little evidence to produce. But we keep the faith because we have learned to trust the processes involved.

By studying the large consequences which followed some small beginnings in the past, we can find encouragement and hope as judgments are made about many of the apparently inconsequential efforts we make today. Campus ministers are being asked today as never before what the mission of the church in higher education is. It is a fair question and it deserves a thoughtful answer. The clue to our future is in our past, in the surprises which rise up to greet us as we tell the story. Already we have reached the point at which we can begin to name some of those surprises.

An Astonishing Story of Success

To review the record of what campus Christian groups have meant to the church and to the world is to be astonished by what they have accomplished, both as student-generated movements and as programs facilitated by trained leadership. That is the overall impression which is created by delving into the history. It is sad to observe that when professional campus ministers gather at the national level today, one does not usually sense the confidence and *esprit de corps* which the heirs of such a story might be expected to display. Instead, there is often a kind of defensiveness, with dashes of anger and cynicism, which says that we are contending with forces beyond our control.

It is my belief that this state of affairs is a legacy from the sixties, a sense that the revolution has come and gone and, after one brief, shining moment in the sun, the status quo has returned with a vengeance. As I have said before, we will return to this important notion as we go along. At this point, we should simply savor the earlier chapters and acknowledge the inescapable truth that the story as a whole is quite remarkable, and that it calls us to a new solidarity with those brothers and sisters whose vision and energy made it so.

I have sometimes heard a veteran campus minister say that the work of the profession has been all but taken over by the universities themselves. Well, yes and no. Yes, because it is true that many of the services first provided by the campus "Y's," such as volunteer service opportunities, hospitality for international students, and vocational counseling, are now standard activities for student-affairs departments. No, because campus ministry is a service enterprise and new occasions teach new duties. If we still had formal responsibility for all the things we have begun, it is doubtful that we could have taken the leadership in the more recent development of biomedical ethics programs, or begun to explore the values arising with technology, as many campus ministries have. We have more than enough to do without lamenting the fact that some of our offspring have grown up and left the nest.

When one reflects upon the Christian presence in American higher education, there is more to celebrate than we can name. Before departments of religious studies in state universities are taken for granted, there needs to be greater recognition of the fact that the Disciples of Christ broke the ice with scores of Bible chairs throughout the country. When we rejoice in the rise of vibrant Christian communities in the Third World today, we ought occasionally to doff our hats to the memory of Christian students like Luther Wishard, Grace Wilder, and her brother Robert, whose youthful hearts burned with zeal for the salvation of the *whole* world. And when we think of the ecumenical spirit which produced the World Council of Churches, the John R. Motts and Ruth Rouses should not be forgotten. Certainly, not least of all, when we observe the Martin Luther King, Jr. national holiday, we ought to breathe a prayer of gratitude for the untold thousands without whose vision and unceasing effort there would have been no colleges whose explicit mission was to serve the national welfare by raising up trained leadership from the black community.

To conclude our reflections on the heritage of campus ministry, I would like to single out a few areas for special comment. I choose them not least of all because they demonstrate how our past speaks to our present condition and points us toward the future. They show campus ministry once more as a kind of *avant garde* in the church and at the same time confirm our instincts toward playing that role today. We will address these issues briefly and return to them again in a later chapter.

To See the World as God Sees It

I had read two major works on the history of student Christian movements before I realized that I did not know the denominational affiliations of any of the chief characters. That was the first surprise to greet me as I plunged into the largely unfamiliar story of the roots of campus ministry in the eighteenth and nineteenth centuries. I realized anew that denominationally based student movements were a creature of the twentieth century. That is not to say that these later developments were a bad thing. What it does say is that there is something about campus ministry, about the idea of a university, about young people themselves, which wants to evoke a larger vision.

The root meaning of the word *ecumenical* is "the whole inhabited earth." It should not be taken as the polar opposite of *denominational*, but as a word which embraces that term along with others, such as *interracial* and *international*. I believe that the desire of students to build a movement, to reach out and make connections with students on other campuses and in other lands, was the result not only of religious impulse but also of the deepest of human instincts: to affirm the essential kinship of all peoples. The absence of denominational consciousness in the development of the "Y's," the Student Volunteer Movement, and the WSCF was due to such largeness of vision.

It would be impossible to overemphasize the importance of the international character of the student Christian movements in their infancy. It is commonplace to disparage the optimism of the late nineteenth century and to dismiss the missionary zeal of the era as mere cultural imperialism. But our very souls are at risk if we yield entirely to such judgments. Ruth Rouse, reviewing her long life of involvement in these matters, wrote:

> Creative imagination and power are released just in so far as the world purpose of God is realized and accepted, and the will of the individual or of the community is brought into line with that purpose. Those alone have clarity of vision who see the world as God sees it.[1]

What would happen in our generation if thousands of students undertook to "see the world as God sees it"? What would happen if in all the churches of America there arose a consensus of opinion to the effect that the only way truly to grasp the reality of the church of Jesus Christ is to experience it in its global dimensions? In this respect, there can be no doubt that the past points the way to the future for campus ministry: internationalization of our vision and experience is essential.

The Early Role of Women in Denominational Work

Am I alone in being surprised by the discovery that "out of 28 college communities in which the Southern Baptists had full-time student secretaries in the college year 1936–37, nineteen employed women workers"?[2] If the rejoinder comes to mind that these were not ordained persons, it must be remembered that, typically, the men were not ordained either. Just as the formation of the YWCA was motivated by a felt need for special work with women students, the denominations early recognized the same necessity. This seems to have been rooted in the fact that women's organizations in the various denominations were strongly interested in foreign missions and in the recruitment of candidates for the mission field among college students. As representatives of the various women's societies visited campuses, they saw the need for the development of leadership roles by women which went beyond recruitment.

In 1919 the Lutherans appointed Mary E. Markley as secretary for work among women students and clearly indicated that her responsibilities went beyond the interests of the missionary enterprise to include concern for the general spiritual well-being of women students. In the early 1920s Agnes Mary Hall was appointed to such a position in the Episcopal Church, and Francis Greenough was chosen for the same role in the Northern Baptist Convention. In 1935 the Disciples of Christ appointed Lura Aspinwal as secretary for their entire national student program for both men and women.[3]

From 1921–29 representatives of various boards and agencies with interest in work among women students formed a group called the Federated Student Committee. The purpose of the group was to develop a united approach to women students by providing a forum where their religious needs could be discussed outside the framework of denominational and organizational agendas. During the twenties, the committee operated a program of team visits to colleges around the country by means of which a group of three to eight staff persons from the several denominations and YWCAs would spend from three days to a week on a campus. They sought to assist local program development, interpret the work of the church to students, and encourage students to become involved in the church's mission. Shedd concluded that the presence of women in leadership roles was an important factor in the development of cooperation rather than competition in many places where established "Y" work and denominational programs were in potential conflict situations.[4]

One is left to wonder why, if women have played such strategic roles for so long, their emergence into the ranks of the ordained leadership of the churches is a continuing struggle. But this is not to suggest that their lot has been all that much better in campus ministry. As late as 1954, eighty percent of women's colleges with chaplaincies appointed males to the post, even when qualified female applicants were available.[5] Nevertheless, it is essential for us to acknowledge the early leadership of women in the developmental stages of modern forms of campus ministry, and to affirm that heritage by the way we plan for the future.

Beginning to Break Racial Barriers

If the attempt to see the world as God sees it even comes close to a proper description of the student Christian movements in their infancy, we would expect to find the issue of racial exclusiveness on their agenda, and this is certainly the case. The only surprise might be in how early, compared to the situation in America as a whole, the student groups addressed the issue. As early as 1922, the intercollegiate "Y's" took a stand against holding any national conference in places where discrimination against black delegates would exist. During the 1930s there was active recruitment of interracial participation in the summer conferences, including one held in Kentucky in 1937. Likewise, according to Shedd, the first national Methodist student conference, held in St. Louis in the same year, was held on the basis of racial equality.[6] In this latter instance there is a very interesting anecdote to report.

In his autobiography the late Howard Thurman describes an incident which appears to have taken place at this very conference. As one of the scheduled speakers at the event, he arrived on an early morning train, was met by a host committee, and taken to breakfast at the Jefferson Hotel, following which he gave the first of two addresses to the conference. When the group returned to the same dining room for lunch, the manager of the hotel refused to serve them, citing a preconference agreement that his establishment would not be requested "to feed or house any

Negro delegates." As a courtesy, he had not pressed the issue at breakfast, but now he would insist that the agreement be honored. If the chairman of the committee wished to take the group to his room, he would serve them lunch there, but not in the dining room. Of course, Thurman refused such tainted hospitality, and when he addressed the conference again in the evening he told the students the sort of agreement their church had made and what its consequences had been.

This story has a happy ending. When Howard Thurman boarded his train to leave St. Louis that evening, he found Harold Case waiting for him. Representing, no doubt, the sentiments of the conference, Case apologized for what had happened, gave assurances that it did not represent the true spirit of the Methodist tradition and vowed that, if ever given the opportunity, he personally would prove that point to Thurman. In 1953, as president of Methodist-related Boston University, Case persuaded Thurman to accept appointment as Dean of Marsh Chapel where he served with distinction until his retirement in 1965. As Dr. Thurman phrased it in his memoirs, he was "the first black man to occupy such a position in the history of the country."[7] Given his lifelong quest to discover and make known the spiritual wellsprings of a universal inclusiveness, the opportunity to serve as religious leader of a major, predominantly white university was critically important to him.

No less so than in the full participation of women in its leadership, or in the true realization of its global character, the church has yet a long way to go in becoming a racially inclusive fellowship. In all these areas, campus ministry has a tradition of leadership which must be affirmed and continued as it seeks its place in the overall mission of the church in the world. Given the astonishing heritage which is ours, such an agenda cries out to be accepted with enthusiasm and hope.

PART II

Overcoming Our Fear of Otherness: A Theology of Campus Ministry

Given the unique placement of campus ministry one would think that it would be a consistent source of theological vitality for the church and, indeed, for anyone interested in a religious perspective on life. Campus ministry is by definition an arena in which the practices of faith have the potential of creative engagement with the intellectual life. I use the word *practices* deliberately in order to make it clear that I am talking about experiential matters and not ideas alone. There is a great deal of talk in colleges and universities these days about "values," and in almost every discipline ethical questions are attracting attention. In some places campus ministers have helped to create the environment in which ethical issues must be addressed. But this is not all that I have in mind when I speak of the theological task of campus ministers.

When I speak of campus ministry as a source of theological vitality, I am thinking in more comprehensive terms. I want to address issues of meaning rather than of values, questions of faith rather than of ethics alone. Obviously, the two things are related; one cannot separate faith from obedience when the frame of reference is the Christian religion. But faith is more than the ideas one finds persuasive; faith is the way one lives into, and out of, the meaning he or she has discovered. Faith involves practices; it is something one does as well as something one believes.

There is a compelling need in our time and place for fresh ways of thinking and talking about religious experience, for a vocabulary of faith which is winsome without being superficial. It may be that the old words are just fine and only need to be used in new ways. Those of us who go about the practice of ministry on an everyday basis in the midst of the academic community ought to have something useful to say in this regard. Although it may never have crossed the minds of those who hired us, campus ministers—at least some of us—should be engaged in ongoing theological reflection based upon our participation in the life of the university.

I believe that creative theological work, as a general expectation of campus ministers, is an idea whose time has come, but it represents a project which ought to begin modestly. The first item on the agenda is the articulation of biblically and theologically informed perspectives on our own work. This is not to suggest that we need a definitive theology for campus ministry in all times and places. Instead, each of us needs to be able to give to the larger church an account which is not only understandable and persuasive but also a useful contribution toward the understanding of mission and ministry generally.

In partial explanation of how his congregation came to be one of the largest in the world, a very influential pastor said, "Birds of a feather flock together." It is a principle espoused by many who have devoted themselves to figuring out what makes phenomenal church growth possible. People want to be with people like themselves. But when I begin to reflect theologically on my long experience in campus ministry, I reach a very different understanding of the church's mission. The key to the future is not withdrawal into sameness, but engagement with otherness; such is the narrow gate, so difficult to enter, which leads to new life in the church.

If the New Testament were read in the light of a veteran campus minister's interests and concerns, what would be the result? If one surveyed the traditional themes of Christian doctrine from the same point of view, what affirmations would rise up as particularly helpful? These are the questions which will concern us in the next few chapters. While we can represent only one campus minister's understanding of the issues, it is a perspective which has been informed by the thinking of colleagues in various parts of the country and in several denominational traditions. Like missionaries who work in unfamiliar cultures, ministers in higher education are confronted at every turn by the phenomenon of otherness. How we respond to this single issue determines the meaning and value of our work, to ourselves, to the university, and, not least of all, to the church we represent.

4

Otherness in the Early Church

When we think about the early church, most of us have a highly idealized picture in mind. Things were much simpler then; all were united in unbroken spiritual harmony and there was such clarity of purpose that persons were willing to die rather than compromise the integrity of the faith. Well, yes and no. Clearly, the first Christians were Jews who were united by their belief that Jesus was the Christ of their expectations. Initially these persons did not experience a radical break with their existing religious heritage; they saw it as brought to fulfillment in new and marvelous events. But this simplicity was short-lived.

We know that in one location these original believers led into the community less orthodox friends who in turn brought along a few Samaritans.[1] While Jews and Samaritans shared some basic beliefs, history had left a legacy of deep antipathy between them. The presence of the Samaritans exacerbated an already uncomfortable situation and led to the expulsion of all who believed in Christ from the synagogue. This separation from the mainline Jewish community made the emerging church even more open to Gentile converts, and intentional outreach to them soon began, most notably in the ministry of Paul.

Although Peter and the other Apostles were initially involved in outreach to the Gentiles, the practice became a source of controversy after Paul began his missionary journeys. Some did not understand how one could possibly grasp the significance of Jesus as the Christ without first being a member of the Jewish community. Organized bands of Jewish Christians went from town to town insisting that any Gentile brought into the Christian community would also have to convert to Judaism and follow its practices.

The issue became so controversial that Paul was brought home from the hinterlands to Jerusalem and a summit meeting of church leaders was held to resolve the problem. On that occasion Paul had the opportunity to explain the nature of his ministry and to argue for its continuation in the presence of some who were quite critical of the enterprise. The meeting ended with a compromise of sorts, but one which asked only minimal acknowledgment of Jewish tradition on the part of Gentile converts (cf. Acts 15).

From the earliest days until the present moment, the church has been troubled by issues arising from the phenomenon of otherness. In the beginning, what to do about first the Samaritans and then the Gentiles was a theological problem which was critical to the formulation of the church's understanding of its mission. Just imagine that the first church-growth consultant was already present to advise Peter that the future of the church lay in the encouragement of a homogeneous constituency and that the decision of the Jerusalem conference had therefore gone against hospitality to the Gentiles! In every age there must be those who encourage the church to overcome its fear of otherness. By virtue of its placement in the pluralistic environment of the contemporary university, campus ministry may find in the category of otherness a distinctive theological perspective for understanding its mission in the world and in the life of the church as a whole.

When debates concerning what to do about the phenomenon of otherness arise from engagement with new constituencies, they represent dynamic moments in the life of the church, full of possibilities for reform and renewal. But, as a human institution, the church easily feels threatened and, falling prey to its survival instincts, acts as though its mission in the world is self-preservation rather than outreach and service to others. The campus comes to be seen as an alien place, the capital city of otherness. At such times, campus ministry feels pressure to justify itself in *conservative* terms, to show how it helps to maintain the strength of the church as an organization. But campus ministry serves the church best when it makes the most persuasive case for greater latitude in its dealings with the Gentiles' contemporary cousins in the university.

The Outsider as Catalyst

One of the great problems of biblical interpretation lies in the fact that what we see in any text we read is conditioned by what we are looking for. We can ask questions of a document which it never intended to address and therefore elicit answers which would no doubt surprise the author. But it is a dilemma which cannot be totally resolved since the intentions of authors long dead, particularly those who lived in cultures quite different from our own, cannot always be discerned. Therefore texts have a life of their own and the interpretation of texts becomes a dynamic process. When I read the New Testament in the light of my experience as a campus minister, I am drawn to aspects of the story which may not be prominent to others. Specifically, I see the relationship between insiders and outsiders as a constant theme of the New Testament and, indeed, of the Bible as a whole.

That Jesus would be born of Mary is presented to us as a highly unlikely turn of events, given her lowly status (Luke 1:48). That the Magi would appear at the manger with their gifts is a surprise as well, since they were Gentile foreigners and therefore not in a position to be looking for the messiah of Jewish expectation. Both these elements of the Christian tradition can be seen as early signs that, when God became flesh and lived among us, there would be many surprises. When the baby Jesus grew up, his first known public utterance would proclaim his identification with the poor and those who are oppressed (Luke 4:16–19). From that moment until his compassionate words to the thief crucified with him, Jesus would repeat again and again his expression of solidarity with the outsiders—with the lost, the least, and the lonely. And, when he died, it was a Roman soldier, not one of the twelve disciples, who said, "Truly this man was a son of God" (Mark 15:39, alternative reading).

People of privilege can quite naturally be expected to resist the implications of Jesus' identification with the poor. But it is not my intention here to fill out the bill of indictment which such a line of thought would raise against us. Instead, I merely want to call attention to the important role played by the outsider in the New Testament and to suggest that our renewed attention to these dynamics is necessary to understanding the potential role of campus ministry in the mission of the church. The outsider, however defined, cannot be understood as merely the object of the church's mission; the outsider must be seen as one who has a contribution to make to the self-understanding of the community of faith. The church needs the outsider.

In his study of the communities which produced the Johannine literature in the New Testament, Raymond Brown shows how the entry of Samaritans into the early church profoundly influenced the distinctive understanding of the nature of Christ which is found in the fourth gospel.[2] The presence of these outsiders forced the church to rethink its understanding of the scope of Christ's saving work. Instead of a messianic figure proclaiming the kingdom of God as expected by the Jewish community, we see the Christ for the first time as a universal presence, the one through whom the whole creation came to be (John 1:3). In trying to understand what was happening in their midst, the church affirmed the perspective brought by the Samaritans that the Christ would be "the savior of the *world*."

If Brown is correct in his interpretation of what happened in the early Christian community which produced the gospel and epistles which bear the name of John, we have a clear example of how engagement with the outsider can stimulate theological vitality. The outsider helps us understand the gospel we preach. Of course, history has taught us that there are dangers in such a process: the struggle to preserve the authenticity and integrity of the gospel is a long and often unhappy story. The church has good grounds for being cautious about taking intellectual risks, but this reticence, while understandable, can weaken the will of the church to engage new publics.

The world of higher education today represents a frontier which both intrigues and intimidates the church. It is in many respects a microcosm of the world and, as such, it is a rich smorgasbord of belief, unbelief, and indifference. But the church makes a serious mistake when it sees the campus as alien territory, a land by nature hostile to its presence. Just as Paul discovered among the Gentiles a large contingent of persons who admired Judaism without actually becoming full participants in its life, there exists in the university today a multitude of persons who have a genuine interest in the spiritual dimension of life, but who are not familiar enough with its practices to consider formal religious participation as a live option. If the traditionally structured local church is all that is available, many of these persons, particularly the students, will remain at a distance. In my judgment, it is one of the principal purposes of campus ministry to provide for these outsiders an alternative means of access to the life of the Spirit.

A constant theme of this book is that the primary task of campus ministry is not to preserve a constituency which is already committed to the church as it stands, but to engage new constituencies in the interest of the church as it is yet to be. Campus ministry ought to be the church with its face set toward the future. Therefore, the celebration of the gospel in the life of the university must find means of expression which are appropriate to an environment which is unique. Somehow, we must understand that the church in its most familiar forms, where things are done in an established and predictable manner, is not necessarily superior to small groups of persons who are struggling, many for the first time, to understand the implications of Christian commitment for life in the academic community. It is the special opportunity of campus ministry today both to help the church understand and claim the many ways it exists beyond itself and to show how this incipient church beyond the church might contribute to the renewal of mission in the mainline denominations.

A Tale of Three Cities

As the name implies, a campus minister is by definition one who owes allegiance to both the university and the church, a situation which is often described as living between Athens and Jerusalem. The former city, having deep roots in ancient classical culture and learning, has its particular understanding of how truth is discovered and communicated. The latter city represents a community which draws its identity primarily from the biblical witness and the tradition of interpretation which has grown from it. It also has its distinctive way of understanding and communicating truth. Simplistically stated, Athens stands for knowledge gained through reason, while Jerusalem represents the truth that is revealed through faith; or, as it is often put, it is a matter of the tension which exists between the claims of the head and the imperatives of the heart.

Obviously, it would be unfair to imply that the church, with its great intellectual tradition, has no respect for the life of the mind, or that the university, guardian of the arts and literature, discounts the importance of the human spirit. Nevertheless, the dialectic at work in the relation between Athens and Jerusalem provides one of the central tensions in the history of the church's life in the world. By attempting to be a citizen of both cities, the campus minister runs the risk of not being fully at home in either. If one thinks of oneself as occupying a house built squarely upon the boundary between two cities, one will constantly be asking oneself identity questions. To which jurisdiction do I really belong? Do I live in unincorporated territory and therefore have none of the protections which citizens can expect from their cities?

To understand the special character of campus ministry, and to place the tension between Athens and Jerusalem into a creative context, we need to introduce a third piece of urban imagery. For this purpose, I propose that we have a look at an ancient city which has not achieved the prominence and recognition it deserves. I speak of Corinth which, in New Testament days, was undergoing a dynamic rebirth. Strategically located on an isthmus, this Greek city lay between two ports and was therefore commercially vital. After having been destroyed by war and lying desolate and uninhabited for a century, Corinth was refounded as a Roman colony in 44 B.C.E. by Julius Caesar. It prospered immediately, and people immigrated to the place from all over the Mediterranean area, bringing with them their native cultures, including a great diversity of religious beliefs and practices.

The most prominent structure in Corinth, aside from the theater, was the temple of Apollo, one of the most revered gods in the Greek pantheon. Through the centuries Apollo had many attributes, among them his guardianship of truth and beauty. Inscribed on the wall of his temple at Delphi were the words, "Know Thyself." But there were other temples in Corinth, including a very popular shrine to Aphrodite, the goddess of fertility. Her cult drew many visitors to the city and helped to establish its reputation for sexual freedom. This city was a dynamic, pluralistic place where all sorts of people with widely differing backgrounds, experiences and values interacted on a daily basis. It was one of the most important cities in the Roman empire when St. Paul arrived as an emissary of the gospel of Jesus Christ in the first century.[3]

Paul's experience in Corinth provides an interesting image for campus ministry. Like a modern campus, the city was an astonishing mixture of people, cultures, ideas, and values. Some people came to Corinth because it was an important place to go if your primary interest was in making money. Some were drawn by the sexual possibilities for which the place had earned a reputation; it was a party city. But it was nevertheless Greece, land of great philosophy, poetry, drama, art, and architecture, the womb of Western civilization. Present as a representative of the young church, Paul lived among the people, sharing their weekday world and trying to figure out how to communicate the

gospel to folks who did not seem to have the background necessary to understand it and who lived in an environment teeming
with alternative ways of thinking and acting.

The mainline Protestant churches today do not have a clear
sense of what campus ministers do or what they ought to be
doing. This is partially because campus ministers themselves do
not always have a clear sense of professional identity and therefore find it difficult to argue their own case in the councils of the
church. I believe that our difficulty in saying precisely what we
are doing in campus ministry is a problem that comes with the
territory. It is clear that, when Paul faced the necessity to explain
his ministry, he had to do some hard thinking and to struggle to
find just the right images to convey what was happening. This
was not because he was confused or uncertain, but because he
was operating beyond the perimeters of the established church,
out there where things are less predictable, where very little can
be taken for granted. But the necessity to understand and explain
the implications of his work was very important, both for him
and for the future of the church. Although no one knew it at the
time, what was happening in Corinth was determinative for the
future shape of both Athens and Jerusalem.

A Corinthian Theology of Campus Ministry

It is ironic that Paul, first encountered by the church as a
menace to its existence, became the theological architect of its
future. After a dramatic conversion experience, he had the intellectual task of reconciling his new faith with a Jewish heritage in
which he was extraordinarily well trained. It is a further irony
that, once he had thought all this through and began to explain it
in the synagogues, the *Gentiles* responded. Having satisfied himself that faith in Christ could be reconciled with his Jewishness,
he then faced the necessity of building a theological case for the
inclusion of Gentiles in the church. The theological vitality of
Paul's letters arises from his constant engagement, in very practical ways, with the phenomenon of otherness.

It is not surprising to find that Paul's brilliant metaphor of the church as the body of Christ, a unity composed of very diverse parts, appears in his first letter to the church at Corinth (1 Cor. 12). It is important to recall that this affirmation of diversity in the church is followed by his beautiful hymn of love in chapter 13: "If I speak in the tongues of men and of angels, but have not love, I am a noisy gong or a clanging cymbal" (13:1). Nothing, Paul says so eloquently, is more important than love which affirms and includes the other. Such literature is the reward for both real engagement with the life of the world and energetic reflection upon the issues which such an encounter brings to the fore.

The pastoral concern with which Paul wrote to those who were young in the faith produced letters which still vibrate with authenticity and power. But it was the necessity of speaking to the saints in Jerusalem, and, most likely, to the church as a whole, which brought forth in the epistle to the Romans Paul's most definitive theological statement. Although it is addressed to the church at Rome, the letter has the character of a general theological position paper, and it is significant that it was completed just prior to his departure for a meeting with "the saints in Jerusalem." I think it is also significant that the letter was written, or at least completed, while Paul was back in Corinth.

While it is impossible to fathom the depths of the great epistle here, its themes will inform the theological reflections to follow. At this point, I would like merely to note that, even when Paul was doing his most profound theological work, it arose out of practical issues associated with his attempt to understand the relationship of Jews and Gentiles in the church. His argument that salvation is the free gift of a gracious God (Rom. 3:24) and that, therefore, there is no distinction in God's eyes between Jews and Gentiles (Rom. 10:12) reminds the church in every age that hospitality should be one of its chief characteristics.

When I read Paul's words in the light of my campus ministry experience, Jew and Gentile do not have a literal meaning; instead, the terms refer to those who insist that faith, at whatever stage of development, be expressed in standard ways, and to those who are unfamiliar or uncomfortable with these ways. When we are called upon, as we should be from time to time, to give to the church at the center an account of our mission, campus ministers should feel a special kinship with Paul and be inspired to use the occasion for theological audacity as he did.

5

With God in the World

The meaning of the Christian faith is closely bound to the peculiar language in which it is expressed. Since we so often speak with persons who are either unfamiliar with, or estranged from, this traditional vocabulary of faith, campus ministers are constantly seeking other words and images which also convey the essential ingredients of a Christian worldview. As important as this task of reinterpretation is, it can be overdone; the farther away from the traditional language we get, the greater the danger that our words will lose their strength. When we go back to the text of Paul's letters and read them with our particular questions in mind, even the most familiar verses have the power to surprise us. Likewise, it is helpful to review the classic themes of Christian doctrine in order to find among them the particular affirmations most capable of providing fresh light on our professional role and of enabling us to interpret its significance for the church as a whole.

God Created the World

That the universe is God's creation is one of the fundamental doctrines of biblical faith which is especially important for campus ministry. Ironically, while a literal rendering of this doctrine causes some to see major conflicts between religion and the scientific theory of evolution, it is precisely the notion of creation which should lead campus ministers to feel at home in the world of the contemporary university. As Creator, God is the Author of all truth; to affirm the doctrine of creation is to endorse the primary enterprise of higher education, which is to discover and communicate truth.

To say such things seems rather simple, but this is not the case. As servants of the God who is the source of all truth, campus ministers are in higher education, fundamentally, as allies of the teaching and learning which are its primary objectives. There is a strong tendency to allow ourselves to feel that we are aliens in the academy, a tendency which is fed by the inherited notion that the purpose of campus ministry is to protect students from influences in the university which undermine faith. While that instinct is not entirely invalid, it tends to insulate campus ministry from real engagement with the intellectual world, and the church is thereby diminished in stature and influence.

The doctrine of the creation leads us to reaffirm the gift of the human capacity for rational thought. Writing from the perspective of campus ministry, Alda Marsh Morgan speaks of the "confidence that reality is such that human intelligence can reliably address and apprehend it."[1] While this point is subject to qualification by other theological perspectives which are equally significant, it is nevertheless very important that this affirmation be made at the outset of theological reflection upon campus ministry. Faith in God as Creator implies that the universe is somehow a coherent whole, and that the more we know about it the better. This is the fundamental assent to the quest for knowledge and understanding which leads the church to affirm the process of teaching, learning, and research, which is the business of education.

A campus minister is present as a friend and advocate of the basic aims of the university, and those who are involved in campus ministry should remind themselves of this fact from time to time. Even so, the feeling of uneasiness will not go away. Not everyone in higher education today will agree that reality is such that human intelligence can discern any sort of "truth" in the sense that religious people use the term. Rather, as Ms. Morgan observes, many in the modern university believe that "an operative grasp of information" is the limit to which inquiry can aspire.[2] For them, the question of truth in a holistic sense is simply impossible or irrelevant.

In some settings this simple affirmation that reality is intelligible will place campus ministry in a prophetic posture in the university. On this basis some campus ministers will find themselves playing the role of advocates of liberal education, holding out for humanistic values in the face of massive pressures to understand education as the servant of the aims of technology. But when campus ministers take it upon themselves to be guardians of the soul of higher education, they will find that they have many allies within the university. Once more, the basic point here is that our faith in God the Creator affirms the importance of education and the role of campus ministry in it.

A Fractured Creation

As the story is told in the book of Genesis, when God created the world and saw that it was a very good place, God felt that the creation still lacked something necessary for the fulfillment of the divine intention for it. So God created a man and a woman, gave them stewardship of the earth, and commanded them to be fruitful and multiply, thus filling the world with people. As perhaps the greatest gift of all, God gave to Adam and Eve the capacity to make decisions, thus giving them a taste of the intoxicant known as power. Quickly, they asserted their freedom to act independently of God's hopes for them, and sin came into the world, bringing death in its train (cf. Gen. 2—3).

We know that this ancient story is true because we have all experienced what it describes in such simple and vivid terms. Even when we know with certainty what is right to do, we do not always do it. Put human beings together in groups, as small as a marriage or as large as a nation, and the problem gets more complex and the consequences more serious. We are very proud beings and our pride leads us to seek advantages in our relationships with other persons. As in the case of Cain and Abel, jealousy becomes a potent ingredient of human relationships, and from that point anything can happen, including murder (cf. Gen. 4).

As Paul wrote to the Romans, all human beings fall short of the glory of God, for which they were created (Rom. 3:23). This fall conditions all of human life and permeates all human institutions. Therefore our affirmation of the creation, upon which we based our enthusiasm for the quest for knowledge as carried on in higher education, is tempered somewhat. All human enterprises, including the university and the church, are flawed by human self-seeking, corrupted by the quest for power which is motivated by pride. This line of reflection becomes complex very quickly, and we have no need to do a thorough analysis here of all that is wrong with either the university or the church. We mention this deep fracture in the human condition to remind us of the need for a strong dash of realism in our assessment of institutions and our hopes for them. Ministry in general, and campus ministry in particular, needs the sobering realism provided by the doctrine of the fall if we are to find our way through the bouts of disillusionment which inevitably come our way.

This is not an injunction designed to urge campus ministers to close their eyes to the sins of the university or the church. The prophetic tradition, so prominent in the campus ministry of the sixties, is still very important in our consciousness, and rightly so. When Presbyterian Ministers in Higher Education adopted a theological position paper in 1985, it indicted the universities as captives of political and commercial powers and accused them of worshiping the idols of "privatism, tribalism, nationalism, and technique."[3] There is ample room for critique of higher education today, and we will discuss some of the more salient criticisms in the pages which follow.

Both of the theological affirmations we have discussed so far are important reference points for campus ministry. We belong in the world of higher education and in the world of the church, or, to continue the earlier metaphor, in the cities of both Athens and Jerusalem. We celebrate the possibilities of both cities, rejoicing in our awareness of God's hand in the creation of both. Human life in this world is God's gift, and it is very good indeed. But, as soon as we say such words, mountains of evidence to the contrary crowd our vision: the world is the scene of outrageous injustice rooted in greed and abuse of power; the catalog of our sins against each other needs no review for any thoughtful person. We cannot place our total confidence in any human endeavor, including our noblest institutions. But, thank God, we have not yet brought from the storehouse the last of our theological treasures.

God's Reaffirmation of the World

At the heart of the gospel is the proclamation that the Creator of the universe came into the world in the form of a human being. This taking on flesh, this incarnation, is God's reaffirmation of the world.[4] The core of the Christian proclamation is the claim that in Jesus Christ God demonstrates that the divine love for the world has not diminished due to human disobedience. In Jesus Christ God participates in our humanity, being made subject to the powers of sin and death. When we know that God is with us, and for us, the untrustworthiness of all human enterprises is less daunting to our spirits. We know that we will fail to achieve our full agenda, but we also know that we will get up and try again and again, and there will be many successes along the way. It is hard to resist quoting Paul's great epistle at every turn: "We rejoice in our sufferings, knowing that . . . hope does not disappoint us, because God's love has been poured into our hearts" (Rom. 5:3–6). In spite of all that has happened and will continue to happen, God is with us and, as in the case of the empty tomb, God will continue to open possibilities where no possibilities are discernible. In Jesus Christ, God reaffirms the essential goodness of creation and continues to take delight in the world and in the possibilities of humankind.

It is at this point that campus ministers reach a theological juncture and have to make a choice—not a "yes" or "no" decision, but a matter of emphasis and style. When one takes a stand in behalf of God the Creator as a basic affirmation, what is the next theological step? In the tradition of the Protestant Reformation, one is likely to follow the idea that God creates with the notion that God also *rules*. The sovereignty of God is a politically potent doctrine and, as in the Reformation, is often raised in defiance of human institutions which have overstepped their legitimate authority. This doctrine was important to the English Puritans, and certainly it was important in the resistance raised by the Confessing Church in Nazi Germany.

What has this to do with a theology of campus ministry? When Presbyterian campus ministers adopted the statement mentioned above, the sovereignty of God was its fundamental affirmation, and that is why it issued such a strong condemnation of the sins of the contemporary university, accusing it of various forms of idolatry. When one looks at the world from the perspective of the omnipotent One and surveys what human beings have done to each other, a certain amount of righteous anger is bound to follow. One finds oneself in the role of the prophet rather than the priest. This is not to imply that the framers of the statement had lost sight of the whole of the gospel; certainly not. But it does say something about where the emphasis falls and about the consequences which flow from that choice.

The contrast is made clear when we examine more closely the distinctively Anglican interpretation of campus ministry articulated by Alda Marsh Morgan. While the sovereignty of God interprets the creation story to mean that God stands *above* the world, the incarnation represents a continuation of creation through God's active presence *within* the life of the world. In the incarnation there is an apparent abdication of God's power for the sake of identification with a fallen creation. To emphasize the incarnation as a primary affirmation is to say that, if the university has sold itself into captivity to the powers that be, it is nevertheless not abandoned. God is present in the world and its institutions, not just in religion and the church. Following this line of thought, Morgan speaks of the importance of "cherishing institutions."[5] In the place of the prophet, one now begins to see the priest standing in the midst of the people as their comforter and advocate before the throne of grace. Again, this is not to say that an Episcopal theology of campus ministry has no place for justice; it is, however, to note where the emphasis lies and the consequences which flow from the choice.

No doubt campus ministers would say that the sovereignty of God and the doctrine of the incarnation are not mutually exclusive; one is not forced to choose one over the other. This is true. But it is appropriate to ask which items from our theological treasure are most appropriately and helpfully brought forward for the enrichment of our understanding in the present situation. In general, I believe that the times are such that campus ministry needs to draw closer to the inner life of the university, to help in the search for clarity with respect to the proper role of higher education in the society and in the world. The university needs criticism and there will be such in the pages which follow. But the university also needs cherishing, needs people who love its hallowed halls and are willing to invest themselves in the revitalization of its liberating role in human affairs.

This discussion need not set up a polarity between the roles of prophet and priest in campus ministry; both are necessary as the occasion requires. Perhaps the tension between the two is resolved in the exercise of pastoral care, particularly when one's concept of the role is broad enough to include assertive caring for the well-being of institutions as well as individuals. It is important that pastoral care be seen not only as "an activity where strength flows to weakness," but also as "the disciplined sharing of strength with strength, the enhancing of what is good, the uncovering of unsuspected beauty, the celebration of faithful work."[6] Perhaps, also, the tension between the theological concepts of sovereignty and incarnation is embraced by another central affirmation: the doctrine of divine grace.

The Graciousness of God

That God is a gracious God is the key affirmation of Pauline theology and is, indeed, the essence of the gospel (Rom. 3:23–24). God shows no partiality in dealing with human beings; all persons are equally valuable in the eyes of God. But this language is so familiar to us that we can no longer have an immediate grasp of its radical character and its far-reaching implications. Such is necessary if we are to have an understanding of the way in which campus ministry lives and moves in the life of the university.

The grace of God is not something that the church can control, nor is God's gracious activity limited to the sphere of the church's influence. Just as Paul found the Spirit stirring among the Gentiles in advance of his arrival, so the grace of God is operative in the life of the university whether or not campus ministers are there to name it as such. James J. Bacik, a Roman Catholic campus minister and theologian, has written:

> God's grace permeates the whole of the cosmos and all dimensions and aspects of human existence. . . . Thus all things are potentially revelatory. Persons, communities, religions, and institutions can all be catalysts for a deeper understanding and appreciation of the divine-human relationship. . . . We approach the university as an institution which is a mixture of grace and sin, just as we experience the Church as saved, but sinful.[7]

I suspect that the contemporary campus is among the more difficult arenas in which to understand the meaning of grace. Although campus administrators continually talk, and quite sincerely, about their desire to build a sense of community, the very form of the university strongly encourages individualism. Regardless of what it says, the contemporary university is a meritocracy, teaching by what it so clearly values most that the race goes to the swiftest. It ranks all who pass through its doors on the basis of achievement, and its understanding of achievement is narrowly defined. Higher education is a system of salvation by works, and as such it values competition more than it values community. One of the most frequently heard words on the campus today is "pressure," and it is heard as often from faculty, particularly the untenured ones, as from students. The pressure arises from the unrelenting commandment to do more and do it better than your peers. Although this paints a very bleak picture of the human environment of the campus, I am not suggesting that it is impossible to achieve community, or at least communities, in the life of the university. It is both possible and necessary, and we will look more closely at this issue in the pages which follow.

Whether or not my assessment of the university ethos is overdrawn, campus ministry is called to represent the God who is, above all, a gracious God. Campus ministry does not import the grace of God from the outside, but affirms that the grace of God is potentially present in the depth dimension of all human relationships, including those which exist among faculty and students, staff, administrators, and trustees. We are present to affirm that the worth of all human beings is grounded in God's love and care for them as individual persons. We are present as a reminder that all human beings are of equal value in the eyes of God, regardless of their grade point averages or publication records. We are present as allies of all who seek to help individuals recognize and claim their own gifts and learn how to use them. As such we often become agents of grace.

But this theological affirmation applies above all to the practice of campus ministry itself. The church all too easily lapses into a polarity between itself and the world; a division which makes the church the sole guardian of the means of grace. To know the grace of God, we seem to say, one must come to the church to find it. Such an assumption is behind our tendency to become preoccupied with the church and see it as the object of our call to servanthood. It cannot be said too often that we are called to serve not the church, but the world; that *mission* is our reason for being. Campus ministry must be understood as a manifestation of the love of God for the world, expressed through the agency of the church. That is why it exists beyond the security of the familiar, and to be faithful to its task must venture into unknown territory. The courage to do this arises from the awareness of the grace of God. A quarter-century of experience in campus ministry has taught me to trust that the grace of God is there, just beyond the boundary of my comfort.

6

Gathering the Church Beyond the Church

The mood of this chapter will be significantly different from the two which precede it. It begins with an autobiographical reflection and moves to considerations which may seem more practical than theoretical in nature. The reason for this is that we will be talking about worship, an activity which by design appeals to our hearts as well as to our heads. But my concerns are nonetheless theological; indeed, the way we approach the subject of worship may be where the great theological divide among campus ministers is located. If what happens at our professional meetings is any guide, the corporate kindling of religious affections is not something we do well.

I know from personal experience the crisis of faith which the college environment can provoke. Once a good liberal arts education, including the critical study of religion, got a firm grasp on my head, it declared war on my heart, a war which lasted for years before the achievement of a still somewhat tenuous truce. Simply put, it was a conflict between thinking and feeling as each sought to claim the dominant place in the house of religion. The day I enrolled in a theological school, my head was firmly in control, so much so that I not only lost the ability to feel the familiar religious emotions but also cast a most skeptical eye on the theological affirmations upon which, presumably, they were based. I could not feel the feelings and I could not think the thoughts of vital faith.

I will make a long story short by recounting a pivotal experience which occurred after that first miserable year in seminary. Out of simple curiosity I went one Sunday morning to observe the pattern of worship in an Episcopal church. As the service began, I was surprised to see how, as the processional cross passed each pew on its journey to the altar, the people bowed; not just a cursory nod of the head, but a bow, however slight, from the waist. For reasons I could not understand, I was profoundly affected by this small gesture and continued to think about it during the service. Given the defensive posture of my mind and spirit, it still seems odd to me that I was seized by an intense desire to be in that place the next time the cross went by and, when it passed the spot where I stood, to bow.

This is precisely what happened. I returned to that church the next Sunday, and when they started down the aisle with the cross I was ready. Although one part of me still hoped nobody was watching, I did it. I bent my body in the presence of the cross of Christ and inside me, way down deep, the dam broke and my spirit surged through, found space again, flowed freely and with great power. Had you seen me at that moment, you would not have known what was going on; I did not know myself. Only with the passage of time did I gain enough insight to realize that I was at that moment getting beyond the impasse of thought against feeling and rediscovering the importance of corporate worship. I had made the first step toward understanding that religious *practices* are as important to vital faith as are what we think and how we feel. That realization has been critical to my life and work as a campus minister.

The Power in the Practices

In a very interesting study, George Lindbeck developed a "cultural-linguistic" theory of religion which, a quarter-century after the fact, helps me to understand what happened when I took my Episcopal bow.[1] He says that a religious tradition may be compared to a culture or a language. To understand either requires submission to certain rules, which is to say there are things one must agree to do in a prescribed way before understanding is possible. One may read travel literature about another country, for example, and gain a certain level of appreciation for its distinctive character. Or one may actually visit the place, see its prominent landmarks, and walk its streets. In the first instance there is an intellectual awareness, and in the second a degree of experiential awareness. But if, as a third option, one submits to the discipline of learning its language, one's encounter with another culture becomes qualitatively different. It was this third way that I had stumbled upon in my rather haphazard quest to recover a meaningful faith.

What I learned when I adopted an unfamiliar religious practice by causing myself to bow in deference to the cross was a lesson which could not be had by other means. Some experiences are just not available without prior obedience to certain rules. In the case of religious faith, there are dimensions of its reality which are known only through its practices. It seems to me that this is a critical insight for campus ministers to ponder. When a Presbyterian or United Methodist campus minister looks longingly at the crowds of students gathering for Mass at the Roman Catholic student center, he or she is witnessing the power of religious practices to go where no amount of merely didactic preaching ever can. For many people, the question is not why to be a person of faith, but how. Access to the practices of faith in an appealing form is a key issue for campus ministry and ought to be so for the church as a whole.

The mainline Protestant churches have declined in membership during an era in which religion itself has become ever more visible and popular. It would not be correct to assume that all the slack has been taken up by the conservative and charismatic churches, although they have clearly benefited from the spirit of the times. Instead, we have the growing phenomenon of the churchless Christian, the person who has an orientation toward belief in Christ, however vague, but does not participate in the practices of the faith, except for attendance at an occasional wedding or funeral. Much of our corporate worship today is simply boring, and it is boring because it is primarily a barrage of words. The person in the pew is not expected to *do* anything; nothing *happens*. A very gifted preacher can partially compensate for a barren liturgy with an ability to create images and recount narratives, but such persons are few.

It has sometimes been suggested to me that worship should not be a prominent feature of campus ministry programs, at least not on Sunday mornings. I am aware of colleagues who have in fact been forbidden to hold such services by bishops, boards, or judicatories of one sort or another. While the reason for this is normally stated in terms of avoiding competition with local church programs, one might also infer that those who hold such views do not want students to have alternatives to the status quo in the near campus congregations. Some have even said, "If they get used to the kinds of things you do in a campus chapel, they will never find a local church that suits them after they graduate." By such comments, well-intentioned persons betray their assumption that the mission of the church is to strengthen itself rather than to serve human need. Ironically, the self-interest of the church would probably be better served if it intentionally sought to foster a variety of opportunities for access to alternative worship experiences. The church would have more *doors* that way, and more people would find their way inside.

Corporate worship is not the only form in which one finds the practices of the faith. There are other spiritual disciplines, such as prayer, Bible study, and social service, all of which are important. But corporate worship is central. I hasten to acknowledge that there are many campus ministers who may not believe what I am saying. They are willing to leave corporate worship to local congregations while they pursue an issue-oriented ministry or, perhaps, a ministry of teaching, social service, or recreational activities. This is not necessarily wrong; everything depends upon how one defines the hungers to be fed. If the purpose of campus ministry is to serve those students who have long been comfortable and active in local churches, there is obviously no need to duplicate resources immediately available in the surrounding community. But if one seeks to serve the campus as a whole, including those with minimal exposure to the faith and those who, for whatever reason, are disaffected from it, alternative access to the practices of faith is critical.

Praying Ourselves Together

In a pastoral letter on campus ministry, the Roman Catholic bishops in the U.S. said that the Christian faith is by nature ecclesial, which literally means that it calls people together. Virtually all campus ministers would affirm that one of their primary goals is to build a sense of community. This is a hope which is shared by a variety of people on university and college campuses. Administrators commonly talk about creating a sense of community among students and faculty. In the absence of regular convocations which involve everyone, such things as athletic teams, residence hall programs, Greek letter organizations, concerts, dances, and innumerable activities are promoted on the basis of their community-enhancing potential. Deans try to counter the impersonality of large classes with smaller, more intimate seminars for freshmen. Everybody, it seems, is interested in community.

For those in the more liturgical traditions, such as Lutherans, Episcopalians, and Roman Catholics, it is self-evident that Christian community is sacramental in nature; it comes together around the altar. Those of us for whom preaching is more central than the Eucharist, and for whom other aspects of the liturgical life have been less prominent, have a bit more work to do when it comes to providing appealing forms of access to a faith community. In an age of electronic imagery and sound, the sermon often seems anachronistic. Certainly, for students who spend a good part of the week listening to lectures, the thought of rising early on Sunday morning to hear a sermon is not particularly appealing. Nevertheless, preaching can and should have the character of event, something which *happens*. When it does, it has the power of a sacrament. There is a great deal that can be done through campus worship as a means of providing access to the practices of the Christian faith.

While most campuses these days—including the church-related ones—have become very pluralistic places, I have found this to be an asset when it comes to teaching the practices of faith through the formation of Christian community. Where Jewish students are present in sufficient numbers to call attention to their observance of holy days such as Yom Kippur and Passover, other students become curious and ask questions about what they are doing and what it means to them. For some, a kind of envy develops which asks, "Why don't we have anything like that?" The truth, of course, is that we do. The problem is that, for much of Protestantism, whatever sense we ever had about the seasons of the Christian year has tended to fade into the vast backdrop of an increasingly commercial culture. Christmas, for example, is *there*, but it is hard to hang onto the sense that it is distinctively ours, a festival which makes us who we are.

I will say again that I see no point in a campus version of what is easily available in nearby churches. But I have found that what is needed in campus worship is rarely to be discovered in local parishes. What is needed is worship which has *teaching* as one of its primary objectives and which is committed to the concept of learning through participation rather than through passive listening. There is a kind of evangelism in this; students (and some faculty and community folks, too) hear, as if for the first time, the good news that they have a history, that they belong to what the creed calls "the communion of the saints." Many on the campuses today have never had such experiences and long for them even when they cannot identify the source of the yearning. By teaching people how to celebrate the cycles of the Christian liturgical year in a campus community, we participate in the formation of Christian identity.

Learning to Trust the Spirit

The second chapter of the book of Acts describes what is

often seen as the birthday of the Christian church. On the day of Pentecost, when those who had followed Jesus were gathered together, the Holy Spirit came upon them. This was in fulfillment of the risen Christ's last words to his disciples before he ascended into heaven, "You shall receive power when the Holy Spirit has come upon you; and you shall be my witnesses . . . to the end of the earth" (Acts 1:8). Sure enough, when the Spirit came on the day of Pentecost, it was known through the power it gave to overcome national barriers. Persons "from every nation under heaven" (2:5) heard and understood what the apostles said as though they were speaking in their own languages. The original genius of the church, as the entire book of Acts so eloquently testifies, was its gift for overcoming the barriers which divide human beings from each other.

One of the strongest incentives for gathering a Christian congregation on a campus is the potential it has for becoming what the Catholic bishops called "a visible sign of the unity of the human family."[2] Local congregations which are genuinely inter-racial in character continue to be uncommon. Congregations which are significantly international in nature are likewise rare. It is fair to ask how the church can bring harmony to the world if it is unable to bring together as many as two cultural groups in common praise of God. I can say from experience that this is not easy to do. But it can be done and there is probably no better place to attempt it than on a university campus. Common worship of God is the place above all others where the fear of otherness can be overcome.

Some things can be accomplished with a student constituency before they can be attempted elsewhere. If, as one example, a campus Christian community works very hard on the issues which must be dealt with in the quest for worship experiences that are inclusive in character, with reference to gender as well as to ethnicity, it may create a model which could inform such efforts in the church as a whole. More immediately, such a community would make an important statement to the campus it serves. And people would begin to judge its relevance by the quality of its life rather than by its size.

Among those who have in recent years devoted themselves to the discovery and advocacy of principles of church growth, some have emphasized the importance of homogeneity: people want to be with folks very similar to themselves. There is no way honestly to deny that this is true. But there is also no way honestly to claim that this represents the best that is in us. In the Christian tradition we know that, when the Holy Spirit comes among us, all barriers of race and class and clan are broken down. That is our faith and our hope for the world. The church exists for the sake of the others, those "other sheep, that are not of this fold" (John 10:16). On the campuses, in urban ministries, and elsewhere, the church beyond the church is born. When campus ministry understands itself in terms of mission, it becomes clear that it exists for those others, however they may be defined.

Liturgy in the Learning Environment

After all we have said about the importance of gathering for the sake of community, it must be acknowledged that such is a lot easier in some places than in others. On a community college campus or at an urban university where the majority of students come and go very quickly as they try to balance getting an education with jobs and family responsibilities, finding a time and place may be all but impossible, even when the desire for Christian community is present. But there may still be ways, if not of forming ongoing relationships, of utilizing liturgical experience in the broadest sense to give expression to the human longing for connection with the ineffable, with the divine depths of human existence which are so hard to contain in words alone.

Ash Wednesday and Good Friday come to mind as prime occasions for ecumenical cooperation in offering worship experiences in or near the workplace for persons who might not otherwise have access to them. Services during the lunch hour and immediately after work may not only attract active Christians who cannot get to their local parishes but also provide a kind of neutral space for the disaffected who may want to test the waters again. On some campuses the lighting of a Christmas tree, with informal singing of carols and sharing of refreshments, is an important tradition. On public campuses, of course, there is a bewildering variety of interpretations as to what is or is not possible in terms of religious observances.

Occasionally, there are national and international events of such consequence that the provision of an opportunity for corporate response is extremely important. When the Challenger space shuttle exploded as millions watched the launch on television, there was an immediate need to gather in groups and make some kind of response, and services occurred spontaneously in places where such had seldom if ever happened before. At the local level memorial services for individuals whose deaths strongly affect students or the campus community as a whole also speak to this deep human need and draw people together across the usual boundaries which keep us apart. The annual Holocaust Memorial service makes an important contribution on many campuses by bringing people together on an interfaith basis for sober reflection upon the consequences which can flow from our tendency to dehumanize those we perceive to be too much unlike ourselves.

When one begins to think about it, there are many occasions when some sort of liturgical response can serve the cause of community building on any campus. For eight years I have led first-year medical students in planning a "Service of Gratitude" to conclude the experience of dissecting human bodies in their anatomy course. While that is a highly unusual circumstance, it serves to remind us that many situations which do not have a formally religious aspect provide occasions for ministry through liturgy. While many of us may resist the numerous calls which come our way to be official givers of invocations, I have come to take such opportunities quite seriously and invest the time necessary to prepare myself to do them well. I have prayed at the opening of a convention of campus food-service personnel, at a national tennis tournament, and on the occasion of the start-up of a new campus telecommunications system, to name a few.

The value and meaning of such experiences is contingent upon how one approaches the task. I can understand how some would resist the role of the ubiquitous invocation giver on the ground that it provides ultimate sanction to mundane affairs and tends therefore to make holy things trivial. I formerly felt that way myself. But now I know that one need not be able to say the long catechism to deserve our prayers, whether public or private. There are experiences shared by all human beings which somehow suggest to us that we have a common Ancestor. We feel this when we gather in large groups and on occasions of beginning (a ground-breaking ceremony) and ending (a baccalaureate service). We feel it when we share a meal or experience a common sadness. In such brief moments we sense that no one is an outsider; however fleetingly, our fear of otherness is overcome.

7

Love Without Limits

As many observers have noted, there is a great contradiction at the heart of American life. On the one hand, our culture teaches us that, although we are immigrants from many lands, we are one people, united in our willingness to make whatever sacrifices are necessary to achieve "liberty and justice for all." But, on the other hand, we are constantly told that to compete with each other in the quest to maximize our material well-being as individuals is what makes our system work. If the rich get richer and the poor get poorer, so be it. Since there is plenty for all, the argument implies, the have-nots are just not working as hard as the haves.

This conflict between the public good and private self-interest has produced a history which swings like a pendulum. Sometimes we see a compelling vision of social justice which moves us to act boldly in behalf of the disadvantaged among us. At other times nothing can sway us from the single-minded pursuit of individual self-interest. It has often been said that the sixties were a time when the public good captured the popular imagination, while the years since have seen self-seeking reign supreme. While the situation is far more complicated than this description implies, it is nevertheless true that the times change, perhaps in a cyclical pattern, and that this vacillation from public concern to private indulgence affects the church and its ministries in higher education.

It is tempting to say that the gospel never changes and that, therefore, the mood of the culture has little bearing upon the way we go about the business of campus ministry. For example, it is hard to imagine a setting in which the meaning of the gospel could be interpreted without talking about *love*. Jesus summarized the Scriptures in a succinct formula of love to God and love to neighbor (Matt. 22:36–40). By the way he lived and by the way he laid down his life, he was himself the incarnation of divine love. St. Paul wrote that love is the greatest thing of all, surpassing in value both faith and hope (1 Cor. 13). No one would argue against the proposition that love is the word which best encompasses what the gospel of Jesus Christ means in any time or place.

If the gospel does not change, it is nevertheless true that our ability to hear it is conditioned by what is going on around us. There is no doubt that the recent dominance of private interests over public concern has made it more difficult to talk about love in a meaningful way. When love is discussed today, it is often in the form of an admonition to love oneself. We are told, even from pulpits, that we cannot love others until we have learned to love ourselves. There is an important truth in this, having to do with our need for a sense of self-worth. But the gospel speaks of a love which does not depend upon how we feel about ourselves in order to make its transforming power accessible. The experience of being loved by Another in an unconditional way is the most direct route to self-acceptance.

To recover the vitality of the gospel today will require theological reflection on love which is serious enough and fresh enough to rescue the word from its popular distortions. Fundamentally, love must be understood as something which necessarily involves somebody or something beyond our solitary existence as private persons. Perhaps we will discover that we can never truly love ourselves until we have learned to love others. If that is not true, what are we to make of the hard sayings of Jesus, the ones that come back to haunt us, such as, "If any man would come after me, let him deny himself and take up his cross and follow me. For whoever would save his life will lose it" (Mark 8:34–35)? These words of Jesus have great significance for our culture as well as for the church.

In its biblical context love always implies relationship with others, life in community, obligations which extend beyond the private self. But today there is a substantial volume of evidence in support of the thesis that our desire for individual freedom is so great that it has overpowered our sense of the necessity to maintain the social context which makes that very freedom possible. If we pursue the matter in Christian terms, we will discover that freedom cannot last for very long in the absence of love. The void which remains after love leaves is always filled by fear, and those who are afraid are not free. This fact is self-evident in any large city in America. It was for this reason that Jesus made the radical claim that we should love not just those who love us, but our enemies as well. Love holds the key to the future not just for the church, but for the nation and the world as well.

Toward Wholeness Through Love

Much has been written about the turn of contemporary students away from complex social problems and toward the more privatized concerns of economic well-being and self-realization. In fairness it ought to be said that, in this respect, students are reflecting the values of the dominant culture where money matters more than anything else. Even though the rest of us may from time to time discount the idealism of young people, when it begins to disappear it is a very unsettling phenomenon. We expect the younger generation to be optimistic because we need their energy and enthusiasm to build the future. Although we cannot do the job alone, campus ministry has a critical role to play in enabling students to transcend the selfish values of a mass commercial culture. Somehow we must reintroduce the notion that service to others is the greatest virtue and the source of the highest rewards which life can offer. Our task is to recreate a vision of the public good which is more attractive than the lure of private indulgence.

In this regard, ethnic minority communities have a great deal to teach the dominant culture, both on the campuses and elsewhere. Ironically perhaps, their exclusion from the mainstream of American life may have helped them to preserve the very values which the nation as a whole now needs to recover and reclaim. From an ethnic minority perspective, the price of full participation in the larger society appears to be the surrender of cherished ties to the family, the community, and the land. When a selected group of campus ministers was invited to write theological reflection pieces on their work, Eradio Valverde, Jr., who was then serving at Pan American University in south Texas, spoke directly to this issue. Serving a campus where more than three-fourths of the students are Mexican-American or, as many prefer to be known, Chicano, Valverde talked about the double bind of the ethnic minority student. Since the university holds the key to economic advancement, Chicanos feel a certain pressure to make the sacrifices necessary to attend. They arrive on the campus as agents of families' hopes and as neighborhood representatives. All relatives and friends are present vicariously through the students and pray that they succeed. Particularly so on a white majority campus, students begin to feel that academic success will involve cultural compromises which amount to betrayal of family and heritage. The dominant culture's emphasis upon individual advancement through fierce competition with others threatens Chicano students' traditional devotion to family and community. They are caught in a psychologically destructive double bind: to succeed is to fail.[1]

The theological category which Valverde finds central to his understanding of campus ministry is that of *wholeness*. Where may I find the continuity between who I am and who I am becoming? In fact, the category of wholeness is an important theological concept for campus ministry generally. Every student who enters a college or university enters a period of personal transition, a time when old values are tested and new values emerge for consideration. Every student encounters in a powerful way the phenomenon of otherness, alternative ways of being and doing which challenge one's familiar assumptions. The contrasts are sharply drawn in intercultural, interracial, and international encounters, and such exchanges therefore hold great potential for personal growth. Since we seem to be predisposed to a self-protective distance at the first approach of otherness, we may become the worst enemies of our own growth.

An administrator with responsibility for minority student programs at a predominantly white university observed that black students on such a campus comprise three groups. Some, by virtue of temperament or previous experience, simply plunge into the mainstream of campus life. Others, primarily those with little past exposure to white majority institutions, quickly withdraw from the threat of an alien environment and seek to minimize their contact with it by concentrating their involvement in the black community on the campus. Between these two groups are those who are struggling with issues of identity, seeking to discover a fresh sense of wholeness which incorporates new ideas and experiences. It should be emphasized that this middle group is very diverse and is not composed entirely of minority students in process of adaptation to the majority culture. Some are taking a step back from their initial embrace of the dominant culture in order to affirm their rootedness in their black heritage.

Although it is not immediately apparent, similar dynamics apply to the experience of white majority students as well. Some have been directed toward the goal of economic success with single-minded determination since the day they were born and see higher education as just the next step on that journey. Others have much deeper grounding in the values of family and faith and arrive anticipating that the college experience will be intrinsically valuable in terms of their continuing development as persons. I believe that most are somewhere in between, trying to figure out how to reconcile their material aspirations with their innate sense that life is more than bread. Again, this middle ground is occupied by students who enter it from opposite directions, and it is the most creative place to be, the place where the real work of healthy human development takes place.

The issues involved in a minority student's quest for identity and wholeness in a white majority environment were already present in the early church. St. Paul, for example, struggled to reconcile his religious heritage with a radically new experience arising from his encounter with the risen Christ. Then his whole ministry turned in the direction of mission to those whose Gentile otherness presented major challenges for thought and interpretation. The situation of Paul is especially instructive for campus ministry because our work, like his, is public in character. Just as he engaged people in the marketplace, our ministry occurs in the weekday world of the campus among persons with widely differing backgrounds, and where the usual potential for conflict is intensified by the fact that students' lives are in transition. Issues of identity and self-esteem are very close to the surface.

When his mission is viewed in a certain way, Paul's theological reflections are a rich source of ideas for understanding the challenge of ethnic diversity in the church. When he wrote to the Corinthians, "So faith, hope, love abide, these three; but the greatest of these is love" (1 Cor. 13:13), he echoed Jesus' summary of the law in terms of love to God and neighbor (Mark 12:28–31). When asked to define the word *neighbor*, Jesus told the parable of the good Samaritan, making it clear that neighbor-love is to include those who are significantly different from ourselves (Luke 10:25–37). Nothing serves the cause of human wholeness more than the experience of giving and receiving genuine love. Campus ministry has no greater task than enabling everyone within the sphere of its influence to grow in love toward God and toward other human beings. The gospel is good news because it proclaims the love of God for the world and for all people everywhere (John 3:16). The power of the gospel to transform human existence is most effective when it comes in the form of other human beings who genuinely *care*.

Paul's experience led him to discover the imagery of the human body as a metaphor for that wholeness which is composed of extraordinarily diverse parts (1 Cor. 12:12–27). For the sake of wholeness, the foot needs the hand and the eye needs the ear; no single part can go its own way and be healthy. Ethnic minority students need the university *and* their particular heritage in order to be whole persons. And so it is with all of us. We cannot truly be ourselves by ourselves; we need the love and assistance of others even as we need to find our own place to stand. In this process, the *other* becomes very important to us. It is essential to remember when we talk about love in the biblical sense that this love is not reserved for those closest to us. Jesus not only asked, "If you love those who love you, what credit is that to you?" but also explicitly said that we must learn to love even our enemies (Luke 6:32–35). Learning to love in such a way is the formula for healthy growth toward wholeness.

Welcoming the Crisis of Change

It has often seemed to me that people, and particularly church people, expect students to grow but do not want them to change. Both campus ministers and administrators have heard the displeasure of parents upset over the fact that their son or daughter began to change significantly after enrolling in college. He or she may be dating someone of a different race or religion, espousing variant political views, doubting previously held religious beliefs, or behaving differently in a myriad of ways. We need constantly to remind ourselves that, while not all change is for the better, one cannot remain exactly the same in attitudes and values if one is to grow. To grow is to change.

Theories of how faith changes by moving through various stages, developed by James Fowler and others, can be helpful in understanding how the crisis of change can be part of the normal process of healthy growth toward wholeness.[2] To understand the theory, it is important to remember that it defines faith very broadly to include whatever makes an individual's life a coherent whole, regardless of whether that person is formally religious or not. The majority of persons espouse a conventional faith: we believe what our peers believe and never subject those beliefs to intense questioning. In college we may find that we are surrounded by people whose faith, while conventional for them, is very different from our own. Once we are in the position of comparing different points of view concerning what is important and meaningful, our lives are open to major changes.

To interact with a person who is significant for us, whether roommate, professor, or friend, and whose values are sharply different from our own can be an unsettling experience, particularly so for a young person. If we have never gone through any kind of self-examination, we can become sufficiently confused to consider our lives to be in a state of crisis. What happens next is of great importance to our growth as healthy human beings. Sometimes people who love us will yield to the parental instinct to intervene and protect us and, in effect, shield us from experiences important to our development. The root meaning of the word *crisis* is to decide or make a judgment, and, of course, the capacity to make independent judgments is the heart of maturity.

The situation of an ethnic minority student on a predominantly white campus is the best available illustration of these personal and social dynamics. He or she is likely to arrive with a strongly developed sense of identity rooted in a particular culture. Suddenly to be in a situation where most people do not share this perspective can be extremely threatening. One response is to withdraw into a small ethnic enclave and attempt to minimize the encounter with otherness. Another response would be to deny one's past and assimilate as quickly as possible into the ways of the larger group. From the standpoint of faith development, the result in either case is the same: one form of conventional faith is traded for another. Ideally, an ethnic minority student will find enough support in the environment to take some risks in behalf of discovering his or her own particular way of being in the world. This is the path of healthy growth and the way strong leaders are formed.

To one degree or another, it is important that every person have experiences of this kind. The encounter with otherness in whatever form is a fresh call to self-examination, learning, decision making, and growth. In such times of transition we are peculiarly vulnerable and therefore have a great need for support rather than protection. Which of these responses they most characteristically offer is a question which the church and its campus ministries ought consistently to consider. Because it requires less of the recipient, protection is often in greater demand than support. How much of each to give, and when, is one of the great challenges for all who work with students.

Love and Justice

The problem with talking about love is that the word is so overused that its meaning tends to dissipate into sentimentality. Love is a warm and cozy feeling as well as a force so powerful that one will lay down one's life rather than betray it. When Jesus used the word, though, it was action oriented: love feeds the hungry, heals the sick, sets the captives free. To love someone is to respond to their needs and concerns. Our calling as persons of faith is to love the world as God loves it, a tall order indeed when we remember that love must be more than an emotion.

Campus ministry has always been concerned with the whole life of the world, from the days of missionary fervor through the civil rights and peace movements of the sixties. This is a legacy which must not be allowed to fade away. Today campus ministers are involved in efforts to influence public policy in favor of nuclear arms reduction and in opposition to apartheid in South Africa. Some of us have been very active against U.S. policy in Central America, while others have taken the plight of our own homeless people as a central concern. Sometimes our attention to such things disillusions potential supporters who feel that we are meddling in politics when we should be devoting ourselves to matters more specifically religious in nature. Where we have neglected the formation of faith communities which nourish the life of the spirit, we deserve the criticism. But truly to know and share the love we have found in Jesus Christ is to have a passion for justice which will not let us rest in comfort while our brothers and sisters in any place are hungry and cold or persecuted by the powers of this present age.

The biggest hurdle to get over in understanding why so many campus ministers continue to espouse unpopular causes has to do with the nature of the relationship between love and justice. Virtually no one in the church would think it wrong to offer a thirsty person a cup of cold water or even to advocate that this be done. But things get more complicated when the issue is moved beyond acts of charity between individuals. For example, opinions would be sharply divided on the question of what to do with surplus food which has been purchased by the government as a price support measure, although no one would argue that hungry people should not have the opportunity to eat. When the issue moves beyond one-to-one acts of charity, the economic status quo is challenged and people begin to get uncomfortable. Our sharpest disagreements are usually not about what goals are desirable, but about how we seek to reach them. Nevertheless, the issue of justice cannot be divorced from the subject of public policy; the decisions we make collectively as citizens have moral implications and there is no way around that fact.

The degree to which the church becomes involved in politics is always a hot topic and, as the 1980s have demonstrated so well, it is not always the liberal wing of the church which is most conspicuously carrying the banner of political solutions to vexing social problems. No one can spell out in advance just how much involvement of the church in the affairs of the state, and vice versa, is good. But we know that the mandate to love our neighbors as ourselves must be followed to the best of our insight and ability, and this mandate will often lead to controversy in the church. While the young certainly have no monopoly on idealism, once they are aroused by injustice they can become a formidable influence for change. A part of their power lies in their lack of experience: unlike their elders, they are undeterred by obstacles which have been written off as insurmountable. Campus ministry is nowhere more faithful to its calling than when it inspires students to seek solidarity with the poor and oppressed, the "least of these" in whom Christ is present in the world (Matt. 25:31–46).

PART III

Campus Ministry as Mission

It would have been reasonable to suppose that, when the first great wave of students born in the postwar baby boom graduated from college in 1968, the churches would reap a bonanza of young adult involvement in their programs. The denominational presence on the campuses was strong, millions of dollars having been spent on new buildings, programs, and staff development since the end of World War II. The expansion of local churches into the burgeoning suburbs had been phenomenal in the 1950s, and a golden age of growth was in prospect as unprecedented numbers of children and youth marched toward maturity. It is a matter of great irony that, after one hundred and fifty years of continuous growth, membership in the mainline Protestant churches began to decline in 1965, and the downward trend has continued ever since. The mere fact that the onset of this membership decline coincided with the arrival of the leading edge of a massive wave of students on the campuses has, I believe, left a largely unacknowledged residue of disillusionment which still colors the relationship between campus ministry and the churches.

I believe that campus ministry today still lives under the

shadow of the great student revolt of twenty-plus years ago, and that we cannot recover full momentum toward the future until we at last move beyond the sixties. Even if, as some suggest, the last decade of the twentieth century returns us to a time of social turmoil and protest, it will not be a rerun of that unique moment in American history. We need fresh thinking about the role of campus ministries now and in the near future, thinking which recovers vital connections with our heritage and restores us to a significant place in the overall mission of the church in the world.

The time has come for the church and its campus ministries to learn whatever can be learned from the most recent era of student activism and begin to focus our attention on the future. Mistakes were made on both sides. Campus ministers too easily baptized every departure from conventional expectations, while local churches maintained their customary caution with respect to controversial issues. The distance between campus ministry and the rest of the church widened, with at least two unfortunate consequences. Some campus ministries became virtually independent of meaningful ecclesial accountability and are now paying the price of a diminished base of support, financial and otherwise. On the other hand, some campus ministries have found numerical success by catering to the strong market among current students for a faith with high promise and low demand.

In the pages which follow, we will review the impact of the sixties on campus ministry, primarily to show how we became separated from certain vital streams of our history and how, for the sake of the future, we must recover some of the tools and structural supports of an earlier time. We must try to find ways of focusing our energy by clarifying what our mission is and by setting realistic priorities for what we will attempt to do in each place. To do so, we need some new metaphors to supplement the modes of campus ministry made popular by the Danforth study twenty years ago.

Finally, I want to suggest some missional priorities for the future which seem essential to me. I want to emphasize the word *suggest* in this connection. I have selected five priorities from a longer list and do not presume to say that the topics I have chosen are exhaustive or equally applicable in every place. I hope it is clear in what I have said in earlier chapters that I also have other priorities, such as communal worship, which I will not mention again. My hope is that my five missional priorities will leave all my readers with questions strong enough to make them say, "I want to discuss this with someone."

8

Getting Beyond
the Sixties

There is no way to understand the situation of campus ministry today without reviewing the broad outlines of what happened during that extraordinary period of American history called the sixties. Since it was an era in which students played a central role, it was a time of tremendous importance for the church's ministry in higher education and, indeed, for the church itself. All other considerations aside, it was an era in which the spiritual dimension of human life was of great interest to the young. It therefore should have brought, long before now, a great harvest of young adults into leadership roles in the mainline churches. But this did not happen. And, because it did not happen, a period of estrangement between the churches and campus ministry began and has not yet been entirely overcome. A better understanding of the era is essential to the restoration of the kind of dialogue which will be in the best interests of the church as a whole.

An Overview of What Happened

The number of students enrolled in American colleges and universities *doubled* between 1963 and 1973. That fact alone is critical to understanding the student generation of the sixties; during that time there were dramatically more young people of traditional college age than ever before. The phenomenon was created by the leading edge of an extraordinary demographic bulge in the U.S. population. Following World War II, the nation entered a totally unexpected, *sustained* elevation of the birthrate accompanied by a period of unprecedented prosperity. The rise in the birthrate began in 1946, peaked in 1957, and fell back to where it began by 1964. The effect was to create a giant wave in the age distribution of our people, containing about one-third of the present U.S. population. Because of its massive size and its impact as a potential market for everything from hula hoops to higher education to jogging shoes, the wave has a major impact upon the whole society as it moves.

From the time they were born until they went to college, the children of the baby boom were socialized in such fashion as to create a generation characterized by extraordinarily high expectations.[1] Almost everything they encountered was new and apparently created for their benefit—houses, cars, schools, churches, shopping malls, toys, and television. It was an energetic, expanding, prosperous, benevolent world, and they seemed to be the center of its interest and concern. They were brought up in an environment in which *their* needs were critically important, and they had every reason to believe that they could control their own future. When they got to college, however, the conditions of life in the world seemed suddenly to be turning against them and, to put it mildly, they were not pleased.

First of all, they discovered that they were going to have to compete with each other to get into the colleges of their choice. Abruptly, it was a seller's market; with such a multitude approaching, admissions offices had not only the luxury but also the necessity of being selective. Once they arrived on a campus, the students were not asked their intellectual preferences so much as, in keeping with established academic procedure, they were told which courses were required and what it would take to do well in them. They would be graded by adults who had the power to divide the academic sheep from the goats. Their social lives would be regulated by established policies while they were on the campus, and so on. Made bold by the force of sheer numbers, the students began to rebel against this regimen of rules and restraints, the likes of which they had never really encountered before, at least not without the mitigating influence of their parents. And they discovered that, when they began to resist, the universities began to change. Course requirements, grading policies, student life environments, and other long-established ways of doing things began to yield to the demands of students. They soon began to have a voice in almost all aspects of institutional decision making.

It is important to acknowledge that, regardless of other factors present in the society, the leading edge of the baby-boom generation was going to create change when it hit the campuses. They had created change from the moment they came into the world, and, when they reach retirement age, they will still be creating changes in the society. This is simply due to their massive numbers and to the way they were socialized as children during the innocent years of the 1950s. But, as we all know, the nation was wracked by profound upheavals just as the campuses swelled beyond capacity with unprecedented masses of students. It was a volatile mix of elements indeed, and the whole culture was convulsed by forces which taxed its ability to remain whole to a degree not seen since the Civil War.

The Roots of the Rebellion

In February of 1960 four black students from North Carolina Agricultural and Technical College took seats at a whites-only lunch counter in Greensboro, North Carolina, and a new phase of the civil rights movement began, a phase in which students were destined to play prominent roles. Through sit-ins, freedom rides, marches, boycotts, voter-registration campaigns, and other nonviolent direct action programs, the most obvious barriers of racial segregation would be overcome, and thousands of students would participate in the process. We need not tell the story here, except to remind ourselves that the civil rights movement continued to be one of the prominent features of American life throughout the sixties.

The rise of a new black consciousness was a part of the ethos of the decade. At some point the civil rights movement ceased to be understood as an attempt merely to guarantee the inclusion of black people in the mainstream of society; it became the vehicle for a new affirmation of blackness, for the realization that many Americans have their ancestral roots in Africa rather than Europe, and that this connection was to be celebrated with pride. This change brought with it a reawakened desire for the academic study of African cultures and the Afro-American heritage in all its dimensions. This new consciousness struck a resonant chord among other ethnic minority groups in America and interest in Hispanic, Asian, and Native American studies grew. A new sense of the reality of ethnic diversity in America became one of the key ingredients of the culture of the 1960s.

The civil rights movement alone, although it was one of the dominant facts of the times, could not have triggered what we now remember as the student revolt. It was the Vietnam War which was the decisive factor. The drafting of young men to go to southeast Asia to fight in a war most neither understood nor approved began just as the number of eighteen-year-olds in the society reached an all-time high. In actual fact, the longest war in our history would be waged by drafting only six percent of those eligible to serve. But the system was such that one had the *threat* of the draft hanging over one's head for as long as eight years, from ages eighteen to twenty-six. Regardless of the odds against having to serve, the students of the sixties lived with the realization that their peers, by the thousands, were being maimed and killed in the war. The Vietnam era gave the children of great expectations their first taste of life as tragedy.[2]

If little in the childhood experiences of these students had prepared them for the disciplines of traditional campus life, absolutely nothing had suggested that the price of being an American might include dying in a war in which the national security was not at risk. If the awareness of racial and economic injustice had not done so already, the war would "radicalize" many thousands of students. The widespread conviction would arise that government and most other institutions of the society were in the hands of an oppressive elite, old men (i.e., over thirty years of age!) with too much wealth, power, and authority in their hands. Inspired by the example of black students who said "No" to racial discrimination through acts of civil disobedience, students of the white middle class rallied in protest against the war, staging massive demonstrations, burning their draft cards, and even forcing the closure of some universities for a time. Those who do not remember this moment in our history may gain some awareness of its seriousness by meditating on the fact that, before it was over, armed representatives of government used lethal force against students in at least three places. Even those students who remained aloof from justice and peace movements had to deal with the specter of their classmates lying dead or wounded at the hands of the state.

There is no necessity here to cover all aspects of what went on in the sixties; the basic facts are well known even if the complexity of the era has not been fully appreciated. The fundamental point is that the student revolt occurred within the largest student generation of our history, and the scale of the disaffection therefore multiplied its impact. The idea arose that the young, not finding the established society to their liking, could simply create their own separate culture in which an entirely different set of values would reign supreme. There was much talk, and not a little action, related to this desire to "drop out of the System."

To complete the picture, we would have a great deal more to talk about. We have not mentioned the essential role of the music of the era or the influence of hallucinogenic drugs. In a desire to foster a "new consciousness" unlike the thinking behind the prevailing norms of American society, Native American and non-Western spiritual traditions became important, as did a rather romantic view of nature and rural life. Alternative communities were attempted from inner-city neighborhoods to rural enclaves. The conviction arose that, were it not for the corrupting influence of society, love and peace would prevail in human relationships. In 1967, when the Haight-Ashbury district of San

Francisco reached the zenith of its influence as an urban, hippie neighborhood, the term "flower children" seemed a natural appellation to apply to its residents.

While all this high-energy activity and experimentation was going on, an old movement was becoming new again and beginning to move in ways which would still be transforming American society after many of the trappings of the sixties were forgotten. Just as black people discovered a new pride in their heritage, there emerged a new consciousness among women and a new resolve to claim all of their rights as human beings. While we can only cite the fact of its occurrence here, the women's movement has touched virtually every aspect of the society, the family no less than the workplace. It is fair to say that, while the struggle is far from over, the new feminism has profoundly and permanently altered American society.

It would be easy to say that the sixties' vision of a radically changed world was merely a naive dream, cruelly crushed, and rather quickly so, by the weight of human decadence. Drugs ruined the lives of many, and the ideal communities they established, at least the urban ones, became scenes of crime, poverty, and disease. Radical factions of the peace and justice movements turned violent, and so on. Even if these charges and more are true, it is nevertheless imperative to come to grips with the enduring contributions of the era. After all, the movement toward the development of a counterculture touched a deeply rooted strain of the American experience, reaching all the way back to the original attempt by the pilgrims to establish a "wilderness Zion" on the edge of Massachusetts Bay. That original American counterculture was to have been so compelling an example of how a human community should live that the reformation of the old order in England would follow in due course.

Americans have never lost this instinct for starting over, making all things new. Through the years we have had our Walden Ponds and our utopian communities; we have them still, although they now attract far less notice. But in the sixties one had reason to believe, because of the massive numbers involved and the possibilities in the electronic media for a revolution of consciousness, that some major social transformation might occur. It was a time when even a few professors from the Ivy League universities achieved fame or notoriety for extolling drug use, becoming devotees of Eastern spiritual disciplines, or writing books uncritically praising the rebellion of youth. In the latter category one thinks especially of *The Greening of America*, written by a Yale law professor who left his prestigious position in order to move to San Francisco and be near the center of the great transformation.[3]

Now we must consider more closely the impact of the era upon Christian student organizations and upon the profession of campus ministry in particular. Just as serious films about the Vietnam War had to wait until the eighties to be made, it may be that we are just now ready to review the most turbulent era in the history of the church's involvement in higher education. We do so in the interest of getting *beyond* the legacy of the sixties, both in the churches and in campus ministries. We must name and claim what is good in that legacy, while at the same time we attempt to lay to rest the issues which have divided us and sapped our energies for so long.

The Fate of Student Christian Movements

In the sixties the term *movement* acquired a meaning which was quite different from what the word meant when we talked about the Student Volunteer Movement of an earlier time. That movement was firmly grounded in evangelical Christian faith. The peace movement of the 1960s was different in that it was composed of persons of varied religious persuasions and of no religious persuasion, who shared in common a desire to end the war in Vietnam. At the same time, strong sentiment arose among student Christians that denominational loyalties were a hindrance rather than a help. The mainline Protestant student movements which had been developed in the forties and fifties merged to create an ecumenical "University Christian Movement" (UCM) in the fall of 1966, an organization which was to be run by the students themselves and not by denominational executives.

The UCM was to be composed of constituent movements at the local level, and on many campuses established groups gave up their denominational identification in the interest of ecumenical mergers. Several denominational professional organizations merged to create the National Campus Ministry Association. Likewise, an ecumenical approach to the assignment of professional staff was widely adopted through the agency of United Ministries in Higher Education, a national attempt on the part of several denominations to achieve a unified approach. Ecumenical councils at the state level were created to administer and support this effort, and the future looked bright.

Unfortunately, the ecumenical enterprise in campus ministry suffered a major setback almost as soon as it had begun. The UCM officers voted the demise of the organization in the winter of 1969. Exactly why this happened is not clear. A simple explanation may be that, in the heady atmosphere of the times, the slow and laborious tasks necessary to institution building were too much to expect of student leaders. But the option of reliance upon adult professionals to do this kind of work was not appealing to students who had demanded the right to make their own decisions in matters affecting their lives. It was simply not a good season for large institutions of any kind. Whatever the full explanation may be, the collapse of the UCM was a calamity of such proportions that we have yet to recover from it.

All of what might be thought of as the infrastructure of student Christian organizations in several denominations, built up over decades, was simply gone, and there was no easy way to bring it back. Regional and national student conferences, for example, which were discovered in the nineteenth century as an indispensable tool in the development and maintenance of the student Christian movement, would vanish from these denominations for twenty years. The high level of commitment to ecumenical ministry would preempt the immediate reestablishment of denominational structures which could have restored such things. A void was created which had theological as well as practical dimensions, and it was simply going to take a long time to get to the place where new foundations could be laid.

The Impact on the Profession

We are very fortunate that a major study of campus ministry was undertaken during the sixties under the auspices of the Danforth Foundation.[4] Although the massive report of the research was no doubt intended to guide us toward the future, its chief value now is its contribution to our understanding of the profound impact of a particular era upon the profession. Kenneth Underwood, author of the Danforth report on campus ministry, drew from the Christian tradition four classic modes of ministry and used them to interpret ministry in higher education: prophet, priest, pastor, and governor. Although it was emphasized that all four modes are important to campus ministry, I believe it is fair to say that the report favored the prophetic mode, reflecting the spirit of the profession at the time the study was done. The phrase *prophetic inquiry* was coined as a key concept, and the suggestion was made that a possible new direction for campus ministry might be the development of programs devoted to research on public policy issues. While not many campus ministry units established formal programs of policy research, the goal of raising public awareness of issues related to social justice and peace was widely accepted as an important dimension of the church's ministry in higher education.

To the extent that the governance mode was understood as a way of calling our attention to how institutional decisions get made, it too had a strongly prophetic flavor, again reflecting the period in which the study was made. Much of the student protest movement was an attempt to change the distribution of power in the university; students demanded a voice in academic affairs, including the hiring and evaluation of faculty. They wanted representation on boards of trustees, and they wanted investment decisions to be made in the light of concerns about peace and justice. They sought, and widely obtained, significant influence in the setting of grading policies, graduation requirements, and the development of courses in new fields of study. In such an environment, the issue of governance had a distinctly prophetic ring to it.

I think it could also be said that even the priestly mode of ministry was strongly flavored by the dominance of the prophetic. Traditional liturgical practices gave way to radical experimentation in many places. Pipe organs and pianos gathered dust as folk, jazz, and even rock music were introduced into campus worship. At Glide Memorial Church in San Francisco, pulpit and altar table were removed from the sanctuary, and flashing images of weekly light shows filled the church. The mood was that of the prophet Amos, "I take no delight in your solemn assemblies" (Amos 5:21). Many of us were influenced by what took place at Glide, and, while the times have changed, much of what we learned about making worship lively, accessible, and inclusive has been of enduring value.

That leaves only the pastoral role, and it also reflected the dominance of prophetic concern. Draft counseling became a large responsibility which fell upon the shoulders of campus ministers during the war years. And we must not forget that the controversial issue of what to do about "problem pregnancies" likewise came our way, as did issues arising from drug abuse. While we attended to the whole range of human hurts, even our pastoral involvement tended to take on a prophetic flavor. The point here is that campus ministry became "movement" oriented; at a time when many feared that the society would come apart at the seams, we were identified in the public mind with those who pressed for change. Since our constituency was a great deal more radical than that of local pastors, some distancing between us and them was inevitable. This tends to be true even when times are normal, and in those days the times were anything but normal.

When we make generalizations about large groups of people, it should be understood that we are not talking about everybody; we are talking about a critical mass, a group large enough and influential enough to set the spirit of the times. Not every student in the sixties participated actively in any dimension of the revolt against the status quo, and not every campus minister espoused the dominance of the prophetic mode. But the generalization holds that the quest for social transformation, for justice and peace, rose to the top of the campus ministry agenda in the sixties and has remained there as, most would say, it should. But the times changed; the age of the student radicals passed into history.

Time to Move On

The 1970s were a kind of cooling-off and settling-down period in American history. The resolution of the Watergate scandal through the first resignation of a president reassured the country that "the System" was, after all, not only strong but also admirable. This new mood coincided perfectly with the celebration of the nation's bicentennial, and patriotism returned in full flower, even on the campuses. Soon it was noted that students were more concerned about jobs than social change and more interested in money than meaning. The phrase makers began to talk about "the new vocationalism" and "the Me generation." Where did this leave the campus ministers whose professional self-understanding bore the indelible stamp of the sixties? Ironically, many of us were in a position similar to that of the veterans returning from Vietnam: we reminded people (in our case, church people) of something they were eager to forget.

But the drift of things in the seventies could largely be explained by the power of economic trends. The escalation of oil prices and the consequent inflationary spiral, along with other complicating factors in the world economy, began their profound and continuing impact upon American life. As the wave of baby boomers hitting the job market began to crest, there were not enough jobs for all of them to do what they hoped to do, even with Ph.D.'s in hand. So the word went to the back of the wave that only the fittest would survive, that the grade point average and resume would seal one's fate forever. The new conservatism among students was a rational response to economic reality on the part of young people who had been conditioned to want it all.

It cannot be denied that, for many campus ministers, recent years have been a time of disillusionment. Their interests, skills, and hopes no longer matched the felt needs of their primary constituency. Some found it easy to focus upon more privatized forms of ministry, such as personal counseling and spiritual direction, both of which resonated nicely with the inwardness which was one of the lasting legacies of the sixties. But neither activity produced the numbers which increasingly budget-conscious denominations began to seek. Many local units found their funding sources beginning to dry up. This was especially true for ecumenically based ministries as financial exigency forced them into competition with agencies which the denominations saw more clearly as *theirs*. Higher education itself continued to change as the average age of students rose and as they became more likely to hold a job and live off-campus. New forms of campus ministry were called for even as the resources available to support existing programs diminished.

How does one committed to a prophetic stance in ministry adapt to a dramatically changed constituency, new generations of students whose world looks and feels quite different from that of their counterparts twenty years earlier? The question is still so important to campus ministry veterans that even those who are new to the profession have to deal with it. They may not have the scars to show, and they may grow tired of the war stories, but, nevertheless, they have to deal with certain institutional consequences of the era. We all do; the church as a whole has to be involved in the process of reconstruction which, thankfully, has finally begun. We are way beyond the time when we should take whatever lessons the sixties have to teach and move on.

9

Missionary Metaphors for Campus Ministry

Campus ministry is at its best when it has a lively understanding of itself as an integral part of the church's mission in the world. In his book *Revolution in Missions*, Willis C. Lamott described the phases of missionary development in a way which has proven to be helpful in understanding differing styles of campus ministry.[1] The origin and maturation of the mission enterprise in any given place typically went through three phases in which the role of the missionary was understood differently. The first phase was that of the *explorer*. The next phase was that of the *colonial administrator*, and the final phase was that of the *fellow citizen*. With a bit of imaginative embellishment, each of these missionary metaphors provides a useful stimulus for thinking about the role of campus ministry.

One of the most famous missionaries of all time was David Livingstone. He went to Africa as a medical missionary in the nineteenth century, but, if you look him up in an encyclopedia, more will be said about him as an explorer than as a jungle doctor. It will be said that he "discovered" Victoria Falls and that, in his search to locate the source of the Nile River, his whereabouts were so long unknown to his supporters back in

England that a search was mounted to find him. He wrote about his travels and provided Britain with its first glimpses of life in the African interior. He spoke out prophetically against the slave trade, and when he died he was given a hero's burial in Westminster Abbey.

The concept of the missionary as a brave and adventuresome spirit, willing to step out into the unknown for the sake of the gospel, presents an accurate picture of the early days of the modern missionary movement. I can myself remember the visits of missionaries to the church I attended as a child. They came laden with the artifacts of exotic cultures and told stories not only about the spread of the gospel in distant parts of the world but also about episodes involving courage and great danger. They were trailblazers preparing the way for others who would come behind them when the time was right and do other kinds of tasks.

The second missionary era was that of the colonial administrator. In such a time, the missionary's sense of identity was clearly with the domestic constituency which sent him or her, and policy decisions and program agendas were likewise set by considerations far removed from the local scene. The missionary supervised the indigenous leaders even when they were more qualified by virtue of experience and insight. In sharing Jesus Christ with other peoples, little attempt was made to separate the gospel from the cultural forms of the missionary's homeland. While there is a familiar stereotype in this image of the missionary, it bears enough truth for us to recognize it as real. When Western cultural forms came with the gospel, the new churches which arose seemed to be colonies belonging to some distant power and therefore aliens in their own lands. This, too, has a great deal to teach us about campus ministry.

The third and most contemporary phase of missionary development is that of the fellow citizen. Leaders realized that the fate of the younger churches which had arisen out of the efforts of missionaries would have to be in the hands of indigenous leadership. As the moral deficiencies of Western culture became more apparent, it was realized that the gospel need not, and should not, be interpreted solely in terms familiar to the cultures from which the missionaries came. Long-range solutions to the problems of ministry would depend upon the outsiders' ability to function within the structures of local societies. It became the part of the missionaries to immerse themselves in an understanding of the native language and culture and to work alongside indigenous leadership as fellow citizens. Only in this way could the real interests of a worldwide Christian community be served.

The Colonial Administrator

Although the word *colonial* carries pejorative connotations which will cause some to think it inappropriately applied in this case, it is nevertheless true that most of our thinking about the nature of campus ministry has not moved beyond the phase of the campus minister as colonial administrator. If we ask, for example, what the church usually expects of a campus minister it appoints to develop a program of ministry at a large public university, a truthful answer will suggest colonial imagery. Imagine a thriving denominational program which occupies a large building across the street from such a campus. An incessant round of activities, including Bible study and prayer groups, worship, volunteer service projects, musical groups, speakers, retreats, and parties attracts the participation of a hundred or more students. The campus minister involved is extremely busy, and in the eyes of the sponsoring denomination such a ministry will almost inevitably be seen as successful. Maybe it is, and maybe it is not; everything depends upon our understanding of the mission of campus ministry.

In the boom years of denominational campus ministries at public institutions, the phrase, "a home away from home" was often used to describe the ambience of, say, the Baptist Student Center or the Wesley Foundation. While the expression can be quite innocent and useful, it nevertheless depends for its effectiveness upon the assumption that the world of the university is an unfamiliar and inhospitable place from which a student will need respite and relief. As we have seen, this was in fact the church's view of the state-supported schools when they first appeared in great numbers after the Civil War. That the world of higher education and the world of religious faith are natural enemies is a point of view which has not entirely disappeared. Of course, there is some justification for the suspicion: learning always challenges our assumptions, including our religious affirmations. The question is whether or not such tensions can be healthy and lead to growth in both knowledge and faith.

None of this is to suggest that the kinds of activities mentioned above are, in and of themselves, not worthy of support. If campus ministries do not do such things, it is a little hard to imagine just what they would do. But the context and the content are critically important. If a campus ministry program is run in such fashion as merely to protect the faith of Presbyterians or Episcopalians or whomever while they are in college, then the image of the campus minister as a colonial administrator, doing the bidding of an agency removed from the immediate environment, is a correct one. Regardless of how many students pass through the doors, no campus ministry which has failed to take a careful look at the university it serves and which has never entered into serious dialogue with the stated goals of the institution as represented in its curricular and extracurricular programs can be considered successful. Unless, of course, the insulation of faith from the challenge of art and intellect is the church's objective in that place.

It is possible for some modified version of the colonial administrator model of campus ministry to be effective in the achievement of goals which reach beyond the simple objective of protecting students from the threat of higher education. George W. Webber, one of the pioneers of contemporary urban ministry, used colonial imagery to interpret the mission of his East Harlem Protestant Parish.[2] In spite of our understandable discomfort with the words, the language can be useful. By definition, the concept of colony has the building of a community as one of its primary goals, and few would argue the point that the creation of community is an essential objective of campus ministry. The critical point is in the nature of the community one hopes to build. Is it simply a gathering of like-minded people with virtually identical backgrounds of class, region, and race? Or is the community motivated by a desire to realize, in at least some preliminary way, the biblical vision of the kingdom of God? In terms of evaluation, everything hinges upon intentionality, upon what we understand our mission to be in a particular place.

The Explorer

At first glance, it would seem that the age of the campus minister as explorer is long past. There is nothing now to compare with Ruth Rouse's journeys in prerevolutionary Russia or with Luther D. Wishard's thousand-mile horseback ride across the Middle East. Is there anything in the missionary metaphor of the explorer which is suggestive for campus ministry today? In fact, the landscape of higher education has changed so dramatically in the last forty years that much of it is territory unknown to the church. Do we really know the world of the technological research institution? Is the church aware of the human consequences of the educational milieu of contemporary schools of law, medicine, or business? Do we know how to relate to the world of the midlife learners, the multitudes who balance family and work with the demands of a couple of courses in a community college? If the campus remains to any significant degree the crucible in which the future is formed, what does the multifaceted world of higher education today ask of the church, or the church of it?

In these days of limited financial resources, days when churches must stretch a dollar as far as it will go, it is highly unlikely that we are going to find a campus ministry equivalent of David Livingstone, dispatch him or her to the California Institute of Technology, and expect a report in two or three years. We are not likely to do that. But we should! We should deploy a select group of campus ministers to a variety of educational settings with no other assignment than to use their theologically tuned eyes and ears. They should start by calling on faculty and administrators and simply asking them what is going on, what the issues are, what is at stake in their institutions at the present time. One would not even have to ask the values question; it would surface in the first fifteen minutes of conversation with almost any faculty member in almost any discipline.

For some reason the churches do not seem to be ready for this level of engagement with higher education. I think it is because we are so preoccupied with our own institutional housekeeping that we do not often see what a golden opportunity is ours in the contemporary university. The first order of business is to look and listen and ask questions. The second order of business is the reporting back, but like Dr. Livingstone before us, we would find the journey so intriguing that someone would have to come and find us. Nevertheless, our stories would be worth the wait; we would discover such an open readiness for an authentic faith perspective that we would scarcely have to debate what to do in response. In contrast to the colonial administrator, the explorer does not bring an agenda from headquarters; the explorer comes first of all as a learner, and that means that one must be comfortable in unstructured situations, in environments one cannot control. In campus ministry today, we must regenerate both the courage and support which the ministry of the explorer requires. Without a new spirit of exploration, we cannot reach the level implied by the third missionary metaphor, the campus minister as fellow citizen.

The Fellow Citizen

The fellow citizen is concerned first of all to understand the language, customs, and values of the place in which he or she seeks to serve Christ in ministry. As the missionary experience teaches, it is more difficult to be a fellow citizen than it is to be an explorer or a colonial administrator; there is less adventure and excitement on the one hand, and less authority and power on the other. The fellow citizen is committed for the long haul, willing and eager to be a participant in the mundane affairs of daily life, to live in reciprocity with one's neighbors. Such is difficult to do in a culture which is not one's own. In addition to acquiring the basic skills of ministry, the fellow citizen must be suited by both temperament and training to function in a specialized society.

Campus ministers have spoken of themselves as "marginalized" persons for so long that they are tired of the vocabulary involved. In the church, but not *of* the church; in the university, but not *of* the university. At its heart, this is not a dilemma but an opportunity. As citizens of the church, we have the possibility of identifying ourselves also as fellow citizens of the university. In doing so, we will discover that the university is not really such an alien place for folks like ourselves. We *can* learn its ways sufficiently well to work in a cooperative way with administrators, faculty, and students, offering our gifts as resources in places where there is very often no one quite like ourselves. I know from my own experience that many doors do not open to campus ministers simply because we do not knock.

The fellow citizen's mode of operation is to enable the development of leadership resources which are already present. He or she has eyes only for the result and not for who gets the credit for its accomplishment. If the university administration can be persuaded to establish a volunteer program of community service or an office to attend to the special needs of international students, so much the better. As we have indicated earlier, the most convincing argument for the success of campus ministry in the life of the university may be the citation of things campus ministry no longer does because college and university administrations have seen their value and taken them over. Personally, I would hate to have responsibility for the student directory or the housing referral service, but I am glad that, when such things were lacking in the early years, Christian associations got them going. The point is that there are new occasions and new duties in higher education today, and many of them have the character of a call to ministry. I say let the church be there and ready to think and plan and work with whomever shares our concern for the welfare of students in particular and higher education in general.

Setting Missional Priorities

Since the word *missionary* has unfortunately acquired negative connotations, some will no doubt resist the application of mission imagery to the interpretation of campus ministry. We have come to think of missionaries as exporters of Western culture, entering other lands for the purpose of saving people from their inferior systems and values. Although some groups no doubt continue to operate in this manner, such is far from a contemporary understanding of mission. Today the term refers to the mission of the whole church in the whole world, and we would like to understand campus ministry as an integral part of that mission. To do so, it is necessary to ask in every particular location what the specific goals of campus ministry should be in that place.

It is clear that the available resources are such that choices have to be made and priorities set for campus ministry programs. In doing so, we ought always to start from the assumption that it is better to do a few things well than to do many things without distinction. Quality is contagious; a program of ministry which is energetic and imaginative will inspire imitation and innovation elsewhere. Lackluster efforts, simply persisting in established patterns with no conscious mission strategy, will compete for ever-diminishing resources as morale spirals downward, compounding the problem. The face of higher education has changed so much that denominational and, where possible, ecumenical task forces should be earnestly discussing what priorities should govern the deployment of campus ministry resources in the closing decade of the twentieth century.

We have mentioned how the federal land-grant program at the close of the nineteenth century radically altered American higher education. With their focus upon technical subjects such as agriculture and engineering, and in their secular character, these large state universities soon displaced the church-related schools from their customary dominance. It was necessary for those who cared about the interaction of knowledge and faith to respond with new ideas and fresh energy and, as we have seen, they did so with flying colors. In recent years the world of higher education has been subjected to vigorous critique for its virtual abandonment of meaningful course requirements in the humanities, fine arts, and ethics. The continuing success of the technological research institutions places still greater pressure upon more traditional schools. The question of higher education's purposes once more cries out for response from those whose special concerns are for meaning and justice.

Many young people who otherwise could not afford to do so are gaining entry into higher education through the community college systems. Perhaps more notably, the parents of such students, and particularly their mothers, are also enrolling in college either for the first time or in the interest of a career change. The colleges themselves have become far more ethnically diverse, and the average age of students has risen sharply. The demand for job-related training has put pressure on many private liberal arts colleges to scale down general education requirements in the competition for tuition dollars. The rising cost to the student and the sinking availability of scholarship assistance have introduced an unprecedented escalation of pressure on the student to make every course one that will make an immediate contribution toward finding a job that pays well. These pressures have created a huge market for proprietary schools which make no pretense of doing anything other than imparting job skills. This is only a sampling of the issues which have changed the college and university scene today and which the church must take into account in setting priorities for its mission in higher education.

In the light of all the circumstances, how would the mission metaphors we have discussed be most helpful in thinking about strategies for the church's ministry in higher education today? Are present programs adaptable to new approaches? By what criteria do we decide that a program is achieving its objectives sufficiently well to merit continuation? Is our primary objective to keep the students in our particular denomination in touch with the church while they are in college? Do we want to have an impact upon the university itself at the level of its policies and programs? If so, would it make more sense to develop a ministry with faculty rather than directly with students? These questions and many more are the kinds of issues which must be faced in setting priorities for campus ministry.

It may be the case that a single campus ministry program will try to embrace elements of explorer, colonial administrator, and fellow citizen styles in its approach to the university. Such would provide a balanced approach in contexts where it is possible. But perhaps in every state, presbytery, annual conference or whatever the appropriate judicatory is, there could be at least one program which is purely exploratory in nature, to be evaluated at the end of a three-year period. In every case, the decision on the style of campus ministry in a particular location will be contingent upon an assessment of what the priorities ought to be in that place. In the pages which follow, I will briefly discuss some important ministry issues in higher education, each of which should suggest a variety of program possibilities. But everything cannot be done in every place. The idea is to make carefully considered choices in order to provide a clear sense of the church's mission on a particular campus.

10

Five Missional Priorities for the Future

It is characteristic of human institutions that patterns of behavior, once established, tend to perpetuate themselves without further examination. Basically, that is what the word *institution* means. But without moments of innovation, times of crisis which lead to change and renewal, institutions are taken for granted and gradually lose their significance. Because its continued existence has lately seemed precarious, we tend to forget that campus ministry is itself an institution and therefore subject to those same tendencies. If there is an atmosphere of crisis in the profession today, it is a situation which is calling forth serious theological reflection which, in turn, is opening new possibilities.

Are we doing things which no longer really need doing? Are we ignoring needs which we should be addressing? Have we done a good job of identifying and making contact with potential allies in the university? While such questions can be threatening, if asked in a right spirit they can put our imaginations in gear and help us begin to see alternative visions of the future. I take it for granted that there are certain basic components of ministry which will be found almost anywhere and that such things do not need to be mentioned in a discussion of priorities. In considering the suggestions which follow, therefore, no one should suppose that they represent all the tasks which are essential to campus ministry. Nor do they represent all the priorities for the future I can think of. Rather, they are offered as important items for consideration, in the hope of stimulating discussions which will lead to a variety of conclusions in a variety of settings.

Evangelism as an Educational Task

If it is not at the very bottom of the list, *evangelism* would have to be among the most unfavorable words one could use in the context of a university. For many, it carries connotations of closed-mindedness and coercion. It signals intolerance and lack of respect for other points of view. Most unacceptably, it seems to be on the other side of the fence from academic freedom. One has only to consider the scandals associated with television evangelists to be reminded of how the word acquired its negative reputation. Nevertheless, can we really be comfortable with any effort to build communities of Christian faith which has no plan for inviting any but the already committed to participate? It is a serious question and one which merits major attention in a discussion of the mission of the church as expressed in campus ministry.

Personally, I reject any suggestion that it is appropriate for a campus Christian organization to seek converts from among students of other faiths. But, if evangelical groups often err in that direction, the mainline groups characteristically err in the other. We have moved too far away from the bedrock affirmation that the good news is something to be shared. Certainly we are correct in our understanding that the gospel is multifaceted and that the quest for social justice is prominent among its dimensions. But, if telling others that they ought to work in behalf of good causes is all we have to say, we have lost the very thing which might motivate them to do so. The social concern of the affluent is apt to miss one important lesson that the poor seek to teach: life is more than bread. The exuberant growth of the church in the Third World says at least that much.

Has there ever been a time when students more urgently needed to hear the word that life does not consist in the abundance of one's possessions (Luke 12:15)? In recent years my eyes have been forced open to the reality that many, if not most, contemporary students have never heard the gospel as an invitation, addressed to them, which merits a response. They are *unfamiliar* with the basic stories of the faith, and they have had no meaningful encounter with the primary practices which sustain it. Careful observers of American life are now saying that biblical illiteracy is so pervasive that it represents a cultural change of major significance.[1]

Although the students of the sixties will always be remembered in part because of their interest in the spiritual dimension of human life, it is important to recall that their interest in such matters did not always include the religious traditions they were closest to. It was more exotic spiritualities which attracted them, from the earth mysticism of Native Americans to a great variety of disciplines derived from Eastern religions. If we recall that popular religion in the fifties came under severe criticism for its lack of substance even while the churches were experiencing the "religious boom," it could be argued that the sixties' generation turned away from mainline Judaism and Christianity in part to protest their banality. In spite of what we read about the growth of conservative churches, there has been a general decline in religious literacy, which began soon after the second World War.

While teaching a literature class a few years ago, I remarked that the story under discussion was similar in important respects to the Parable of the Prodigal Son. Seated before me in a semicircle were about a dozen very bright students from affluent families, articulate young people whose abilities qualified them for admission to a selective college. At the moment, they all looked at me with blank expressions on their faces. A few questions confirmed that no student in the class could remember ever having heard the Parable of the Prodigal Son, and none had a clue concerning who its author might be. After I had described this episode in a speech, a woman who taught in one of the most prestigious prep schools in the land told me that she had had an identical experience with a reference to the Parable of the Good Samaritan. It is possible to grow up in America with an otherwise superb education and never hear the two most familiar stories told by Jesus.

The central formative struggle in my own life has been an attempt to come to terms with the limitations of my religious upbringing and work my way through to a more mature religious faith. In contrast, many students today are the sons and daughters of parents who are themselves virtually illiterate in religious matters. These students therefore have no tradition to kick against as they seek to define their identity with any kind of ultimate reference. They do not know the stories and practices which point us in the direction of spiritual depth and meaning, with the consequence that they are beginning their journey as adults quite unprepared to meet the intensity waiting for us all in both the really good and the really bad experiences of life.

Mainline campus ministries must reorient themselves to a situation in which we cannot assume that people in general, faculty and staff as well as students, possess even rudimentary knowledge of the Christian faith. Programs designed to nurture the already faithful who enter the foreign land of the university may continue to be important, but they will not be an adequate response to the challenge which the environment raises. Likewise, calls to participation in the struggle for peace and justice based upon a mature understanding of the biblical witness will increasingly fall upon deaf ears. The explorers must be sent out looking, listening, and asking questions in the hope of learning how the spiritually deprived may be fed and clothed.

Regardless of whatever alternative words may be found for it, the question of evangelism must be at the heart of the discussion of the church's mission in higher education. Because of its well-deserved connotations, I do not like the word at all, and my use of it is intentionally provocative. What I hope for is a consideration of the issue in the light of the university as a kind of spiritual wasteland, a place where folks are increasingly unaware of the church rather than hostile to it. I am convinced that a part of the answer is a vigorous program of education in which people are made familiar with basic information about the Bible, Christian thought, and the practices of a faithful life. But we must not forget that a sense of wholeness, meaning, and purpose cannot be sustained by ideas and information alone. We must learn how to kindle the affections again, and that takes us into the realm of prayer, worship, and art. It is a matter of central importance to our work.

The Recovery of Vocation

One of the central questions faced by young adults is, "What shall I do with my life?" It is an important question in situations where it is reasonable to suppose that one has enough options to require a choice. In late twentieth-century America it has become the all-consuming question for most young people and certainly for those in the middle class and above who have reason to believe that their opportunities are abundant. Further, in recent years a variety of factors have converged to extend the question from youth to middle age and beyond. The large-scale entry of women into the work force (some after years as full-time parents), the necessity or opportunity which many adults have for second careers, the emergence of new occupations, the pressure of financial exigency, and other factors are causing people to ask again and again, "What shall I do with my life?"

In the 1970s and 1980s, the severe critique many aimed at youth was that they had framed this critical question in exclusively economic terms. The job came to be viewed as the single door to a future worth hoping for, and schools of law, medicine, and business were deluged with applicants, while interest in teaching, nursing, and social work waned. There were many reasons for this development, which were obscured by the journalistic rush to label students as "the Me generation." In truth, the cost of higher education had risen so much as to force many into such indebtedness that making a lot of money as soon as possible after graduation seemed essential. Nevertheless, it is true that the question of life goals came to be asked in terms of the economic fate of the individual rather than in terms of the larger needs of society.

The rediscovery of the concept of vocation is a much needed counterpoint to the current obsession with self-fulfillment. As James Fowler and others have pointed out, the fulfillment of the individual has lately been defined in terms which preclude its realization.[2] Self-fulfillment, understood as freedom from all externally imposed constraints, sets one over against the claims of family, tradition, and community. But it is these very things which provide the context within which the deeper meanings of human existence are found. One of the major gifts ethnic minorities are bringing to the larger American cultural mix is their insistence upon the importance of family and community and, in some cases, the significance of attachment to place and land. One cannot satisfactorily answer the question "What shall I do with my life?" without reference to realities which go beyond simple self-interest.

The idea of vocation is that one makes life choices in response to a call which comes from outside oneself. Traditionally, the call arises when the assessment of one's gifts takes place both in the context of awareness of the needs of the world and in a mood of openness to the promptings of the spirit of God. Our daily work is not to be seen as a necessary evil or as merely a means to an end, but as a medium through which God and the neighbor may be served. This is not to suggest a sentimental glorification of the routine and tedious nature of many jobs, but to affirm that daily life can be lived with a spiritual dimension which lends dignity to work. It is not necessary that one's vocation be the same as one's job; some find it necessary to work at one job in order to be able to spend other hours doing what one loves and feels called to do.

There are many ways in which campus ministry can make important contributions to human development and meaning through the concept of vocation. The most effective way to assist young people in the discovery of vocation may be to put them in touch with older persons who are established in occupational roles which are of interest to young people, and who attempt to maintain the inner dialogue between faith and work. Some very enterprising campus ministry unit might develop an internship program in which students are assigned to work with persons who are strong role models for Christian vocation and who, for that reason, would take seriously the opportunity to serve as mentors. The potential for building ties with local churches in this way would be another attractive feature of this topic. The program possibilities in the concept of vocation are many, and the need is demonstrably great.

Education for World Citizenship

It has been said that one of the reasons for the apparent self-centeredness of students over the last decade or more is their belief that the world is locked into an unchangeable trajectory toward nuclear annihilation. In the face of long-term catastrophe, they hope to fence off a little space of their own and enjoy as much as they can for as long as they can.[3] It is hard to argue with their assessment of the trends: the gap between the haves and the have-nots continues unabated; the destruction of the natural environment is a global phenomenon; senseless wars rage on year after year; economic chaos looms on the horizon. It is a world so out of balance ethically that multimillion-dollar devices prolong the lives of the aged few while thousands of infants die from chronic diarrhea. In the midst of all this and a great deal more stands the nuclear capacity to destroy humanity many times over. Why fight a losing battle?

This assessment of the trend of things is hard to deny. But people of faith believe not only in the grace of God but also in the resiliency of the human spirit. What is needed today is a renewal of vision, the capacity once more to imagine a world in which peace and justice prevail. And that is possible. Human beings have an unquenchable thirst for hope. The task right now is to get more of us to look up from our private agendas just long enough to see each other again. The shock of recognition will come, and we will remember that the destinies of all are linked by unbreakable bonds. In the most profound sense we are all family, all children of one God, and given the right circumstances we all know that this is true. It is vision we need, both in the sense of the ability to see each other and the capacity to imagine an alternative future.

Education for world citizenship clearly belongs among the top priorities of colleges and universities today, but such a commitment is unlikely to become commonplace anytime soon. Nevertheless, the resources are there in abundance. There are concerned faculty in many disciplines who are both willing and able to bring important perspectives to bear upon almost any issue of international significance. Perhaps more importantly, the presence of persons from other lands, including Third World countries, has grown significantly on almost every campus. There is no substitute for the effectiveness of first-person encounter in raising our consciousness of how the policies of our powerful nation affect the lives of persons struggling to achieve a better life in other lands.

Campus ministries are strategically placed to serve a catalytic function in bringing together university resources on issues of international significance. If we take the matter of apartheid in South Africa as one example, it becomes clear that among political scientists, historians, economists, and others there are those who have much to contribute to a discussion raised in the interests of justice and peace. The question of nuclear arms policy, as another example, invites the engagement of natural scientists with political scientists, theologians, ethicists and so on. It is often a matter of who will take the initiative in surfacing these issues in a public way, and that is clearly a role which campus ministries are equipped to play. In doing so, we make an important contribution to the educational process.

Some campus ministry programs have long organized work projects in developing nations as a way of providing students with firsthand experience of life in another culture. If this is done without paternalistic overtones and there is real engagement with the people, such experiences can be life altering in their impact. At campus ministry professional meetings and student Christian conferences, efforts are being made to underwrite the expense of international guests who can share their perspectives. Everything that fosters our sense of a global common destiny, and particularly those things which help us to realize the worldwide character of the church of Christ, is of primary importance today.

As we have seen, the great national and international student conferences in the late nineteenth and early twentieth centuries profoundly touched the lives of thousands of students around the world. We have also seen how the collapse of the UCM in the 1960s broke the continuity of that history. It was not until the eighties that sufficient momentum had gathered to call our students together again on a national basis. Some who were not part of UCM had continued to meet: Lutherans, Southern Baptists, and the Intervarsity Christian Fellowship held such conferences, some quite successfully. But Roman Catholic, Presbyterian, Episcopal, and United Methodist national conferences began again only quite recently.

When large groups of people meet together for a common purpose, their collective reality is somehow greater than the sum of its parts. This is a truth which has been known from the dawn of history; there is a power in numbers which can rouse us for good purposes or ill. To gather student Christians from every part of the U.S. and every corner of the globe is to create a new reality. We discover that the church is somehow more real than we thought, more full of energy and hope; our own spirits rise and we wonder what we might do next.

I am quite sure that those of us who are involved with campus ministry today have the opportunity and the responsibility to rebuild a network of student Christian movements which is as wide as the world. All of the necessary infrastructure must be reconstructed, and there is therefore a great deal of work to do. Some things may have to go undone for the sake of this effort; in the long run it will prove to be the better investment of our energy and resources. Intercollegiate meetings of state, regional, and national scope will have to be built from the grass roots level toward the realization of a global student Christian fellowship. The impact of such a movement will be greater than our most fervent hopes for it.

Ethnic Minority Ministries

In the late 1980s a story appeared in the press about a Harvard student who, although he was doing well academically, confessed to having robbed more than a dozen businesses while at home during vacation periods. Here was a handsome young athlete who had made nothing but "A's" in high school and who had picked Harvard from among the half-dozen or more elite universities which had offered him admission. Why was he throwing it all away?

The rest of the story is a narrative of the excruciating pressures felt by a student who had grown up in a Los Angeles barrio, the son of parents who had immigrated to the U.S. from Mexico. In his words, he could not bear the contradiction between his good fortune and the lot of his parents who were working hard and making sacrifices in his behalf. His criminal behavior served two purposes: it enabled him to contribute immediately to the economic betterment of his family, while at the same time restoring solidarity with the friends he had left behind in the barrio, many of whom had dropped out of high schools, joined gangs, and staged robberies as a kind of macho ritual. While this brilliant young man could do well academically at the top of the Ivy League, in a cultural sense he could find no place there in which to stand; he could not be a whole person.[4]

First, let us acknowledge that this is an extreme and therefore unusual story, even though it followed by only two years a similar episode involving a gifted black student who was killed by police in New York City in an alleged robbery attempt. Thousands of ethnic minority students do well in the best universities and colleges from coast to coast. But the unusual character of these events should not obscure the lesson which they teach: to varying degrees, "the best and the brightest" of ethnic minority young people face a very difficult challenge to their identity when they first enroll in white majority institutions. All the familiar stresses which any student feels are multiplied and intensified for them.

Most of us are familiar with the dilemmas facing black students on white majority campuses, and we are becoming much more aware of the Hispanic presence among us. As I write these words, a petition is circulating on the campus I serve, drawing hundreds of supporting signatures, which asks for the establishment of an Asian Studies program. Korean, Chinese, and Indian students overcame whatever traditional tensions exist among them to make common cause in behalf of learning opportunities which would enhance the distinctive heritages of Asian-American students. The U.S. is still very much in process of discovering the implications of its commitment to liberty and equality. It is a challenge which falls with special relevance at the feet of those serving in the name of Christ on the contemporary campus, where the reality of American pluralism is met face to face.

Every campus ministry unit serving a white majority campus should continually ask itself what it can do to serve the welfare of ethnic minority students. Years of experience have taught me that a white campus minister can play an important enabling role in improving the campus environment and resources for those whose cultural heritage tends to get short-changed in a variety of ways. There is an obvious and compelling need for more ethnic minority persons in campus ministry. Until that happens, a great deal can be done by the rest of us. Particularly so when we understand that ministry with ethnic minority persons is a two-way street: they have gifts to share which, when the opportunity is there, will enrich the life of the campus as a whole.

Issues of Human Sexuality

Our sexuality is so basic to our human existence that it is difficult to discuss any aspect of it with objectivity. Our identity, for good or ill, is heavily conditioned by a complex fabric of genetic inheritance, childhood experiences, and other factors. Most of us, at some level, are locked in a struggle to come to terms with the conflict between the desire to discover our own individuality and the role expectations defined by our culture. While women have lately won some major victories in the long quest to overcome the limitations placed upon them by gender stereotypes, their emergence raises more sharply the question of the victimization men have visited upon themselves by clinging to exaggerated notions of what maleness means.

It is not possible to say a great deal here about the movement of women to cast off the imposed restraints of traditional role expectations and find their rightful place as full partners in the human journey. Although there is clearly a much longer way to go, revolutionary change has already occurred and the overall movement toward equality and justice maintains its momentum. But the church is not exactly leading the charge, and we have more to do inside our own camp than elsewhere. The civil rights movement taught us that getting to the lunch counter was a hollow victory if nothing on the menu was appealing. It is not enough just to get the door open; one must be able to come in without parking one's identity outside. In the case of the women's movement, this means winning the opportunity not only to exercise power but also to do it in ways which may break the precedents set by men.

These issues are difficult enough without considering the fact that we are distinct from each other not only in terms of gender but also in terms of what is commonly called "sexual preference." That is an unfortunate phrase because it implies that everyone makes a choice in such matters and feeds the argument that our sexual orientation is the result of a personal decision loaded with moral implications. It is highly unlikely that one's primary sexual orientation is a matter of simple preference. The deck is surely stacked by biological, psychological, and social conditions which none can control. That so much of the church's sentiment remains in willful ignorance of these facts, and that, by policy and practice, the church reinforces conditions which distort the lives of homosexual persons, is disgraceful (i.e., it denies "this grace in which we stand" [Rom. 5:2]).

I suspect that campus ministers have more contact with individuals who identify themselves as homosexual persons than local pastors do. This is not only because our work takes place in the weekday environment of a great variety of people, but also because we are perceived to be less identified with the defense of traditional prohibitions which are associated with religion. In this case, I mean the denunciation of homosexuality by both the state and the church. As long as we do not have face-to-face encounters with persons we perceive to be radically different from ourselves, it is easy to dehumanize them, to see them as loathsome objects rather than as persons. If my assumption that campus ministers have more open contact with them is true, we are in a position to work toward greater understanding of homosexual persons in the church.

Our advocacy of greater understanding and acceptance of homosexual persons is made both a great deal more difficult and a great deal more urgent by the fact that the dreadful disease known as AIDS has spread most rapidly among gay men. This development has fueled the fires of homophobia and caused the more insensitive among us to feel confirmed in their estimate of homosexuality as the depraved choice of individuals to violate the law of God. But it has also called forth a compassionate response to human suffering which might open the door to greater understanding and reconciliation. All I am suggesting at this point is that, among the pressing issues related to human sexuality, the discrimination which homosexual persons experience is a question of justice which ought to be of particular concern to the church's ministry in higher education.

As with all the other topics for the future which we have discussed, the whole range of issues related to human sexuality is far too broad and complex to be addressed here. But it is astonishing to realize how little is available in the education of the young to give them sound guidance in understanding these matters so essential to human happiness and fulfillment. In all my years in higher education, for example, I have seen very little in the way of formal education with respect to marriage and family life or how to build and maintain relationships of intimacy and trust throughout one's life. There is more to do in this regard than we can name, and the hunger for it is definitely there. Campus ministers must be among those who take issues of human sexuality with seriousness and try to respond to the many needs which are associated with this complex subject.

By virtue of its primary association with the rising generations, campus ministry by its very nature participates in the inevitable tension between the old and the young. While controversy for its own sake makes no sense, disagreements which arise in the quest for a better society and a more faithful church ought always to be welcomed. It is my hope, and my fervent prayer, that the issues raised in this book lead to healthy dialogue about the mission of the church in higher education. Jesus' words about reaping where we have not sown the seeds are profoundly true in the life of the church (Matt. 25:24–26). We are all the beneficiaries of the courage and work of those in earlier generations who created the phenomenon which we now call campus ministry. Having gleaned so much from their labors, we must now take our turn at the task of sowing fresh seeds.

Notes

Introduction

1. "Empowered by the Spirit: Campus Ministry Faces the Future," a pastoral letter by the U.S. Conference of Catholic Bishops (Washington: U.S. Catholic Conference, Inc., 1986), p. 4.

PART I

1. Brendan Gill, *Here at the New Yorker* (New York: Random House, 1975), p. 77.

Chapter 1

1. Clarence P. Shedd, *The Church Follows Its Students* (New Haven: Yale University Press, 1938), p. 222.
2. Clarence P. Shedd, *Two Centuries of Student Christian Movements: Their Origin and Intercollegiate Life* (New York: Association Press, 1934), pp. 1–2.
3. Ibid., p. 15.
4. Cf. Martin E. Marty in *Context: A Commentary on the Interaction of Religion and Culture* (Chicago: Claretian Publications, 1986), pp. 3–4.
5. Shedd, *Two Centuries of Student Christian Movements*, p. 36.
6. Ibid., p. 62.
7. Ibid., p. 102.
8. C. Grey Austin, *A Century of Religion at the University of Michigan* (Ann Arbor: University of Michigan, 1957), p. 27.
9. Frances Helen Mains and Grace Laucks Elliott, *From Deep Roots: The Story of the YWCA's Religious Dimension* (New York: National Board of the YWCA of the U.S.A., 1974), pp. 12–14.
10. Austin, *A Century of Religion at the University of Michigan*, pp. 8–28.
11. Mains and Elliott, *From Deep Roots*, pp. 15–16.
12. Ruth Rouse, *The World's Student Christian Federation* (London: S.C.M. Press, 1948), p. 27.
13. Shedd, *Two Centuries of Student Christian Movements*, pp. 137–50.

14. Ibid., p. 258.
15. Ibid., p. 275.
16. Ibid., p. 362.
17. See Ms. Rouse's own account of her work in *The World's Student Christian Federation.*
18. Shedd, *Two Centuries of Student Christian Movements*, pp. 391–92.

Chapter 2

1. Cf. James H. Smylie, "Roads to Our Present," in *Church Related Higher Education*, ed. Robert Rue Parsonage (Valley Forge, PA: Judson Press, 1978), p. 151.
2. Kenneth Underwood, *The Church, The University, and Social Policy* (Middletown, CT: Wesleyan University Press, 1969) p. 51.
3. Seymour A. Smith, *The American College Chaplaincy* (New York: Association Press, 1954), p. 4.
4. Ibid., p. 12.
5. Smylie, "Roads to Our Present," pp. 152–54.
6. Jacqueline Fleming, *Blacks in College* (San Francisco: Jossey-Bass, 1984), p. 4.
7. James Farmer, *Lay Bare the Heart: An Autobiography of the Civil Rights Movement* (New York: New American Library, 1986), pp. 117–33.
8. Fleming, *Blacks in College*, pp. 150–53.
9. Shedd, *The Church Follows Its Students*, p. 5.
10. James C. Baker, *The First Wesley Foundation* (Nashville: Parthenon Press, 1960), pp. 18–24.
11. Austin, *A Century of Religion at the University of Michigan*, p. 15.
12. Shedd, *The Church Follows Its Students*, p. 56.
13. Austin, *A Century of Religion at the University of Michigan*, p. 16.
14. Shedd, *The Church Follows Its Students*, pp. 124–25.
15. Thomas R. McCormick, *Campus Ministry in the Coming Age* (St. Louis: C.P.B. Press, 1987), p. 47.
16. Ibid., pp. 6–20.
17. Ibid., p. 40.

Chapter 3

1. Rouse, *The World's Student Christian Federation*, p. 93.
2. Shedd, *The Church Follows Its Students*, p. 159.
3. Ibid., pp. 155–57.
4. Ibid., pp. 160–63.
5. Smith, *The American College Chaplaincy*, p. 159.
6. Shedd, *The Church Follows Its Students*, p. 150.

7. Howard Thurman, *With Head and Heart* (New York: Harcourt Brace Jovanovich, 1979), p. 169.

Chapter 4

1. Raymond E. Brown, *The Community of the Beloved Disciple* (New York: Paulist Press, 1979), p. 35.
2. Ibid., pp. 35–40.
3. Jack Finegan, "Corinth," in *The Interpreter's Dictionary of the Bible*, ed. G. A. Buttrick, et al., 4 vols. (New York: Abingdon Press, 1962), pp. 682–84.

Chapter 5

1. Alda Marsh Morgan, "Matter Made Articulate in the Divine Praise," in *Invitation To Dialogue: The Theology of College Chaplaincy and Campus Ministry*, ed. Robert Rue Parsonage (New York: National Council of Churches, 1986), p. 67.
2. Ibid., p. 73.
3. "Ministry in Higher Education: A Presbyterian Theological Perspective," an unpublished statement adopted by Presbyterian Ministers in Higher Education at their annual meeting, Lewis and Clark College, Portland, Oregon, June 22, 1985.
4. Morgan, "Matter Made Articulate in the Divine Praise," pp. 64–65.
5. Ibid., p. 66.
6. Ibid.
7. James J. Bacik, "Campus Ministry: Theological Reflections from a Catholic Perspective," in *Invitation To Dialogue*, p. 85.

Chapter 6

1. George A. Lindbeck, *The Nature of Doctrine: Religion and Theology in a Post-Liberal Age* (Philadelphia: Westminster Press, 1984), pp. 32–41.
2. Cf. "Empowered by the Spirit: Campus Ministry Faces the Future."

Chapter 7

1. Eradio Valverde, Jr., "Christ, Chicanos, and Campus," in *Invitation To Dialogue*, p. 155.
2. See James Fowler, *Stages of Faith: The Psychology of Human Development and the Quest for Meaning* (San Francisco: Harper and Row, 1981).

Chapter 8

1. Cf. Landon Y. Jones, *Great Expectations: America and the Baby Boom Generation* (New York: Ballantine Books, 1980).
2. Ibid., p. 102.
3. Cf. Charles A. Reich, *The Greening of America* (New York: Random House, 1970).
4. Underwood, *The Church, The University, and Social Policy*, pp. 79–96.

Chapter 9

1. Willis Church Lamott, *Revolution in Missions: From Foreign Missions to the World Mission of the Church* (New York: Macmillan, 1954), pp. 28–35. This book has been utilized in two previous studies dealing with campus ministry: Phillip E. Hammond, *The Campus Clergyman* (New York: Basic Books, 1966), p. 8; and Henry E. Horn, *Lutherans in Campus Ministry* (Chicago: National Lutheran Campus Ministry, 1969), p. 30.
2. See George W. Webber, *God's Colony in Man's World* (New York: Abingdon Press, 1960).

Chapter 10

1. See, for example, Allan Bloom, *The Closing of the American Mind: How Higher Education Has Failed Democracy and Impoverished the Souls of Today's Students* (New York: Simon and Schuster, 1987), pp. 56–57.
2. James W. Fowler, *Becoming Adult, Becoming Christian: Adult Development and Christian Faith* (New York: Harper and Row, 1984), pp. 97–105.
3. Arthur Levine, "Today's College Students: Going First Class on the Titanic," *Change*, March 1981, pp. 16–23.
4. Robert Lindsey, "A Wasted Chance: From Barrio to Harvard to Jail," *The New York Times*, July 26, 1987, sec. Y, p. 12.